heal your soul

heal
your
soul

practical ways to inner peace

clare wilde

KYLE CATHIE LIMITED

First published in Great Britain 2001 by
Kyle Cathie Limited
122 Arlington Road
London NW1 7HP
general.enquiries@kyle-cathie.com

ISBN 1 85626 406 8

Text © 2001 Clare Wilde
Illustrations © 2001 Juliet Dallas-Conte

Senior Editor: Helen Woodhall
Copy Editor: Anne Newman
Designer: Mark Buckingham
Production: Lorraine Baird and Sha Huxtable

Clare Wilde is hereby identified as the author
of this work in accordance with Section 77 of
the Copyright, Designs and Patents Act 1988.

A Cataloguing In Publication record for this
title is available from the British Library.

Printed and bound in Singapore by Kyodo.

With love to my husband

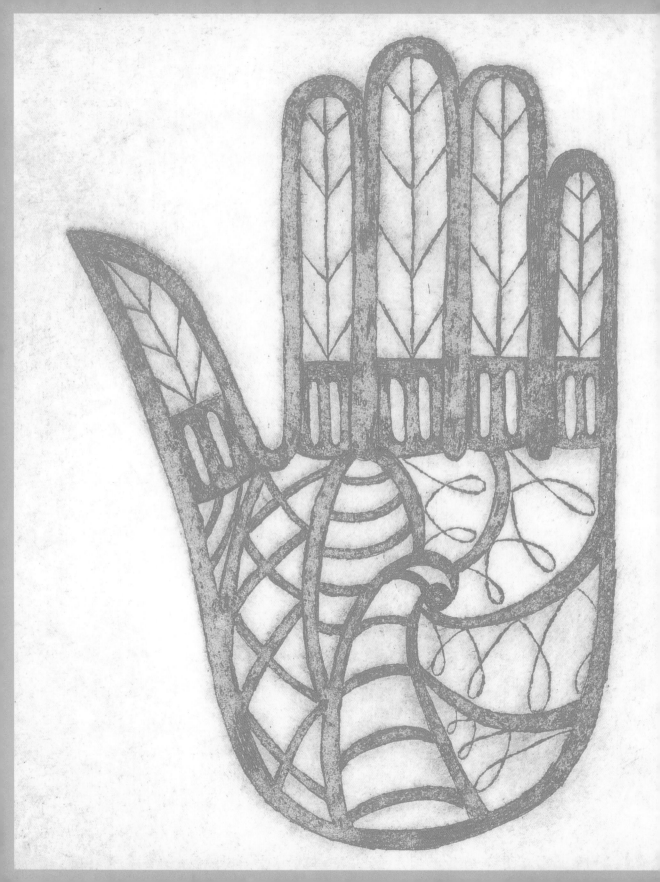

Contents

Healing your soul is all about letting go. It's about finding out who you really are and living your life in a healthy, vital and meaningful way. You may have picked this book up because you're feeling tired — not just in 'a-good-night's-sleep-will-fix-it' way, but really tired of the way your life is going. Most of us, at some time or another, would have described ourselves as feeling soul-weary, and looking for a

Introduction

way to recharge and revitalise. You may be unwell, or you may be looking for a holistic approach to improving your health and wellbeing. You may be a therapist whose interest in this book is professional, or perhaps you are reading it because you're experiencing emotional turmoil, and are looking for ways to find some peace. It may be that you feel you are at a crossroads in your life, that things are not going well for you, or that you are simply searching for something more than you're currently experiencing. Whatever your motivation for wanting to learn more about healing, I hope to offer something that can take you a little further along your path, and closer to the essence of healing that each of us holds within.

YOUR HEALING JOURNEY

In these pages you will find a practical guide to healing at soul level, beginning with your own life and health as it is and seeing it for what it could be. From why and how you got here, and where you are now, to what you need to heal, and how to do it. This book offers an integrated approach to touching your

soul energy, through exercises in perception and awareness, vibrational medicine, meditation, and visualisation, to help you to reach a whole new level of consciousness.

Healing is all about listening to your soul. It is about finding out who you really are, and making that your reality. In a society where everyone is sick and tired and looking for something other than a shallow, materialistic existence, here is a way to answer that deep, unanswered need that drives us all constantly to seek answers to the eternal questions – Why am I here? What am I doing? – and to let us begin really living. *Heal your Soul* will guide you through a process that will enable you to realise your connection with your true self and the world around you, and to walk your soul path. It offers a straightforward approach to this deeper shift in healing, going beyond the symptomatic treatment of the physical body and the must-do-better approach of mind-body medicine. We will look at the simple truths behind healing holistically from the level of your soul, through your own journey, and in making this journey, you will not only benefit yourself, but learn to raise the awareness of and heal those around you. The new shift in healing is away from the healer and the healed, towards healing from within. Looking inwards for your own wellbeing is a straightforward process that everyone can engage in through an empowering and freeing approach. Each of us can learn to get in touch with the energy of the soul and listen to the flow of energy within the world around us. In so doing, we raise our awareness of who each of us really is and learn to be healed within the wholeness and peaceful energy that lies at the eye of the human storm.

THE HEALER WITHIN

Not long ago, healing was something that was 'out there'; something that someone else did to you, or for you. Now, however, healing has found its way back into the common domain. We have become just a little more concerned with taking care of ourselves than previously, and it is no longer seen to be indulgent to want to take care of our own minds and bodies. Rather, it is seen as an essential part of living a happy life. Many of us now look to therapies for the body and mind a little more closely than we did before, in a search for a deeper form of healing. This is a reflection of the onion-peeling ethic of the times in which we live, showing that we are no longer happy just to look from the outside, but are intent upon peeling away the layers to find out what's really going on inside.

A huge shift is taking place, largely through the new forms of communication and dissemination of information that technology has made available to us. It has been said that knowledge is power. However, while the ability to understand and act upon knowledge in a useful way can indeed bring valuable growth to the lives of others, just having knowledge or information means nothing at all, unless it is shared – and that is the essence of our times. The once firmly closed doors of elite educational institutions are being thrown open, and covert societies are publicising their principles and practices. Governments and even the Vatican, that most private of all private organisations, are making public some of their most closely guarded secrets. Put simply, knowledge that has hitherto been kept in the tightly closed fists of the few is now being made available and even shared freely with the masses. This shift is, of course, just as it should be in what has become the age of the common man's quest for spiritual enlightenment, and in this spirit, this book is for anyone and everyone – for anyone who is interested in

Many of us now look to therapies for the body and mind a little more closely than we did before.

healing and raising their awareness as part of the aquarian age.

In response to mankind's development, the healing and therapeutic movement is undergoing a shift of its own. Healing is no longer in the domain of holy men, wise women and silent sages. Therapies and bodywork are something we can all do for ourselves and for each other – no more myth and magic, no more flowing robes, just healing, pure and simple, in all of us, from all of us and for all of us. It should therefore

DAVE – A SELF-CONFESSED MR AVERAGE

Dave is a salesman who developed an interest in healing as a result of his own personal health issues. He suffered from stress and tension-related back pain for some years and had exhausted all forms of conventional healthcare and therapy including heavy-duty painkillers, osteopathy and physiotherapy, before turning to complementary therapies such as acupuncture and reflexology. His reflexologist mentioned that she felt his pain was stress-related, which sent Dave to the nearest bookshop for to carry out some research. He read about mind-body medicine and found various therapists and teachers along the way, eventually learning a form of healing therapy for himself so that he could treat his own back from both a physical and mentally oriented, holistic approach.

Dave is a self-confessed Mr Average. He works in an office five days a week, drinks beer and watches football with his mates. He also attends a regular healing circle, treats people and animals in his spare time, and has taught his wife Sue, a shop manager, to heal. Sue uses her healing skills to help Dave with his back (which incidentally gives him no pain these days); with their son, Alex, their cat Jake and with her plants in the garden. Dave hopes to leave his nine-to-five job soon, and to work full time in healing. But few of his colleagues would ever have guessed that he is looking for a deeper meaning to his life than just his selling targets, and making a wage. Until, that is, someone mentions that they have some back pain, or a football injury, and Dave is there in the coffee break with his 'magic hands' and the offer of a book on self-healing to read.

Dave gradually realised that his lifestyle was the cause of his stress, and thus his back pain. He felt as though, at a very deep level, he was a square peg in a round hole – he wasn't really doing what made him happy. He got right down to the level of his soul – of who he is, and what he wants to do with his life. As a result, Dave and Sue have found that their interest in healing has not only benefited their health, but has led them to look at ways of slowly but significantly changing the way they live their lives. They eat more healthily, they recycle their household rubbish, they have moved to a more spacious and less oppressed area, they think more positively, have a more fulfilled relationship with each other, and overall they live with a deeper sense of peace. As Sue puts it, 'Now, Dave and I just laugh at the ridiculous things that would have caused an all-out row before. After a while it dawned on us that we were only making ourselves miserable. That even applies to the job Dave's been doing all these years, to earn the money we thought we had to have. We just said – we don't need to live like that. We don't want the pressure and the strain any more.'

come as no surprise to you when I say that no special tools, skills, or training are needed for you to be able to heal yourself or others: you are your own best healer. You are your own guru, your own expert. All it takes is the willingness and intent to heal.

HEALING FOR THE COMMON MAN

So what does all this mean in real terms? Every day, in my healing and awareness workshops, I meet people of all ages, from all walks of life, who, with predictable regularity, tell me the same things: 'I've tried everything, but still my physical symptoms return'; 'I've had so much therapy of different kinds, but still get stressed and upset'; 'I just don't feel at peace'; 'There must be something deeper, something more than this'. These words come from ordinary people, from different backgrounds. The message is that, yes we can all use aromatherapy bubble bath, take a herbal dietary supplement and maybe get a reflexology treatment from the next-door neighbour when we feel the flu coming on, but where is the real healing? What is the key to finding out where the sickness really comes from? How can we prevent these same conditions from recurring, again and again? Questions such as these have driven me to write this book.

Once you begin to investigate healing, and ask these questions about your own life, you may find yourself walking a different path from the one you have hitherto followed. Sooner or later, through the search

Once you begin to investigate healing, and ask these questions about your own life, you may find yourself walking a different path from the one you have hitherto followed.

for a deeper understanding of ourselves, questions and thoughts about holistic healthcare lead on to more spiritual matters. It is then that searching questions begin to emerge, such as 'Why am I here?'; 'What am I meant to be doing with my life?'.

Before we go any further, consider this: simplicity is the essence of all healing. There is no great mystery, there is no one and nothing 'out there' that can find your healing for you. True healing is within you, and has been all the time, but it means letting go of all the conditioning, the words, the beliefs, and the experiences, that may have led you to believe that you are anything less than whole. The essence of this book is to help you to find simple ways to release whatever is holding you in an unhappy condition. Within each of us there is a place where we are whole and at peace and where we CAN let go of all the other junk; *Heal your Soul* provides the key to that place.

WORRYING YOURSELF SICK
'Making ourselves miserable' is something we are all guilty of more often than we would probably choose to admit! At the time, it seems so important to win the argument, prove the point, finish the project, gain the attention, earn the money. Each of us tends to believe that we are somehow invincible – that we can take so much misery because the pay-out is worthwhile. But now it's time to be more honest about who we really are at soul level and to acknowledge our limitations. By making ourselves miserable, all we're

doing is choosing to affect our minds and bodies in ways that are less than healthy or positive. And in fact, all of that takes us nowhere but further down the slippery slope to un-health and dis-ease!

So, there is nothing more encouraging than seeing other people who have made the changes we need

Within each of us there is a place where we are whole and at peace and where we CAN let go of all the other junk.

to make ourselves, and how their lives have improved as a result. Without exception, each of the people I have worked with has come to learn about healing through an event or person in their own life who would not take 'no' for an answer. They might have been led by someone close to them who needed help, an unwell pet, or their own health issues. And without exception, they have all begun to ask those probing questions; 'Why did this really happen?' How did the sickness come?' There's a deep knowing in all of us that there's more to the human condition than meets the eye; and that there's more to sickness than just a bug or a virus. How come some of us get the cold that's going round, and others just don't? Your GP will probably tell you that most of us succumb to sickness due to mental stress. But what can we do to alleviate that stress in the first place? Ultimately, it comes down to either making some changes in your world, or in the way you see and feel about it. That's where the deeper healing, the deeper sense of peace, really come from. You don't have to change your life physically, if that's not what you feel you want or need to do; sometimes it is as easy as looking at life a little differently.

HEALING IS WHERE THE SOUL IS
The people I have worked with have all been on their own journeys to find the deeper sense of peace, the place where the healing really is. *Heal your Soul* is a product of working alongside them as they set out on their own healing journeys, to reach the very centre of their own being — the soul. I am privileged to be part of these very personal journeys of exploration, these quests for the knowledge to heal, and to be able to offer what we have learned together here, in this book. Use it to help propel yourself, as part of the community of mankind and as mankind heals itself, along the next steps in the process of our evolution and growth through the new era.

The information in this book will

Without exception, each of the people I have worked with has come to learn about healing through an event or person in their own life who would not take 'no' for an answer.

resonate with you on many levels, because I have written it from the hearts of those I have worked alongside in healing workshops and on an ongoing basis in life. The changes in modern society that have precipitated the movement towards soul-level healing are symptoms that we all feel every day. Shallow values, an emphasis on materialism, money and appearance have left us all feeling separate, isolated and utterly disconnected. Much of the current shift in awareness, the 'new consciousness', is driven by this emptiness in a search for something more. But the age of the guru is now gone, and we must all look to the guru within, because that is where true healing is, and always will be. This book will reflect your own journey and that of your inner guru, showing you how your true self becomes the teacher, healer and master of your own life.

We'll begin our journey on a straightforward physical level, with healing for the body. Then, we will progress to the realms of the mind, where healing encompasses everything from the hands-on to the 'must-do-better' mind-body approach. Finally, we will take a good look at the real wizard – the little guy behind the curtains who is pulling all the levers. We will reach

the place where the healing really lies, and we will touch your soul. That's the place where your peace and health are, and that knows precisely and exactly what each of us needs to do to heal.

We will reach the place where the healing really lies, and we will touch your soul.

ALCHEMY IN YOUR OWN HOME
What we will be dealing with here is the age-old practice of spiritual alchemy. We'll be turning lead into gold, transforming the rough stone into the smooth and polished. Forget the garret laboratory and Einstein hairdo – you can work this magic on your very own sofa, and even keep your slippers on! The simple premise behind soul-level healing is that each of us knows who we really are and what we're here to do.

So much of life is a compromise. Well, you can compromise, you can change things; or, you can change the way you see things, and far from being something you need someone else to do for you, soul-level healing is best and easiest to do for yourself.

Always remember that this is all very simple. It's all about letting go.

Healing from your soul, finding your path, getting 'on purpose', and on flow with your life is not about discipline and flogging, striving and working. Of course, there is effort to be made, but the essence of the process is about peeling away your layers of conditioning, and allowing your natural inclinations to come through. It's about taking the time to listen to your Self, and to understand who and where you are. It's a very gentle process.

Heal your Soul also reflects man's developmental journey – from physical through to spiritual – both in terms of human evolution through the ages and in terms of our own lives, as an example of man as the microcosm reflecting the universal macrocosm. So, let's take the first step on the journey of mankind as he learns to heal himself, beginning from where you are now.

Forget the garret laboratory and Einstein hairdo – you can work this magic on your very own sofa.

CHAPTER 1

Agenda

The concept of the energetic soul as the core of the living being is one that sometimes has religious overtones, but it isn't something you have to firmly believe in, in order to benefit from the practical work in this book. The traditional concept of the soul is as a vital spark of energy; a little piece of the greater, overall creative energy that is considered either as the divine, or as an atomic, quantum creative soup — what Einstein called the unified field. This is the level of energy where creation actually takes place. It's where waves of light become sub-atomic energetic pockets, which collectively form atoms, which collectively form matter. All matter, whether living or apparently inanimate, is composed of atoms and can thus be thought of as simply slow light. Scientists struggle with the 'paradox' of seemingly opposite states of energy, the particle and the wave, but this opposite of states is the fact of creation of the 'whole' in nature. In other words, something must have opposite aspects in order to be a whole (there would be no dark without light, no cold without heat). So at a basic level, all matter is interconnected and is, in fact, the same.

This is where science is leading the spiritual revolution back to where the Rishis, the ancient spiritual masters of the Ayurveda, sat, cross-legged, emphasising the understanding that 'we are all one'.

WHERE WE ARE ONE

Sub-atomic 'particles', as they are known, or the slow-light energy that goes to form atoms and thus matter, also have a dynamic energy or 'consciousness', of their own. If you observe or influence a sub-atomic particle or pocket of energy, it will actually change its behaviour as though in response to being

The principle of influencing matter through our own intent and being, is a powerful tool for healing.

observed. Other particles or pockets of energy will react as if they, too, know that the first one has been observed. Scientists sometimes describe this reaction to influence from outside as the level at which energy has its own consciousness; without consciousness, the world as we perceive it would cease to exist, and so would we. This is a powerful image to bear in mind when you begin to address your own healing. Because everything in our world is made up of this energy/particle state, each of us has the ability to interact

with everything around us and thus influence our world, not just in terms of healing, but in many other life-changing ways. We can change our own existence through the formidable power of our own intent by calling into being, through our own creative process of thought, action and deed, whatever it is that

we choose to experience. For example, if I choose to pick up my cup and drink my tea, I first have the thought of drinking, then I direct my hand to lift the cup, then I drink the tea. I could equally have chosen to give the tea to my dog, or to place the mug at the top of the lane. True, drinking tea is hardly a life-changing issue, but the principle of influencing matter through our own intent and being, is a powerful tool for healing, as we shall see later.

The ability to work with energy in this way is something that has fascinated man throughout his evolution. There was a time when, functioning purely in an animalistic way through our ancient, basic, 'lizard' or limbic brains, we all perceived the energy surrounding us and were simply a part of the energetic makeup of our surroundings, very much as animals are today. As mankind evolved and began to question and become conscious of his actions, the 'seeing is believing' culture dulled our senses to the point where those who healed or had remarkable powers of intent were seen as somehow strange and different. Very often they were people who lived close to nature, and who, having become feared by Christian cultures, were hunted or killed as witches. Healing and energetic powers were sanitised and sanctified and taken into the hands of organised religion and a privileged few. The sub-atomic 'light soup' is the healing, creative energy that cultures have historically named in different ways, and revered and praised as an all-powerful presence.

SCIENCE – THE NEW GOD

Scientists have thus come full circle – from an intention to 'prove' that our world was purely mechanical, to an understanding of the world as a vast field of energy, of matter as energy, energy as information, and space/time/matter/energy as infinitely directional! Now, we're finding out that as our awareness increases, we are all healers, and we can all work with energy to heal our own bodies and minds just as well as those around us who we would formerly have perceived to be experts. Whichever way you look at it, there is a form of consciousness, innately interconnected throughout all matter, that drives the formation of anything that exists – rock, bird, tree, air, dog, water, and you and me. Each of us, as human living matter, has a level of conscious, living light as the life-

The idea of each of us as a miniature element of the universal whole is also a way of expressing humankind.

energy of our being – and this is what can be thought of as the energy of your soul.

The idea of each of us as a miniature element of the universal whole is also a way of expressing humankind, or each individual being, as a tiny reflection of the greater scheme of things – man as the microcosm, or individual whole form, of the universe as macrocosm. This is why some of us tend to think of the soul as an actual energetic entity in its own right; almost like a little ghost that mysteriously leaves the greater whole energy source and 'enters' or joins with the physical body as we are born into this world.

We begin our physical existence on this planet with a certain amount of intrinsic, characteristic personality.

That same soul then 'leaves' us as we die and returns to the greater energy source – a little like the cycle of raindrops coming from and returning to the ocean.

THE CENTRE OF YOUR WORLD
Another way of looking at the concept of the soul is as a name for an aspect of the human psyche that is deeper than anything we normally use and access; not just the subconscious or unconscious, but an entirely 'other' aspect of

consciousness. This could also be called a state of higher awareness – where you're functioning from a place of stillness and knowing rather than one of worry, mental chatter and noise. It's the state we try to reach during relaxation and meditation exercises. It's a place where we feel utterly centred, and still, and at ease, where our brains slow to somewhere between alpha and theta wave, around 8.8hz, which is also the frequency at which the earth is said to be audible. It's almost as if we are merging our consciousness with that place of creative, divine, loving energy as we enter that state. This is also the level that we reach when working with energy to heal, and sometimes when we're deeply relaxed – in the bath, or when dropping off to sleep. It's what I call the 'eureka' state, where we know all we need to know.

Psychologists and those who study the development of the mind explain that the soul aspect of our personality is that which is innate to us; that with which we are born. We begin our physical existence on this planet with a certain amount of intrinsic, characteristic personality; with a knowing, drive and feeling, which is the essence of what we truly are as individuals. This is not so far away, in fact, from the traditional concept of the soul as 'coming into' the body of the child at birth, with its life's work already planned, agreed and mapped out. Sometimes it is thought that the soul energy is so very immense and powerful that much of its' innate knowing is eclipsed at birth, so in effect, we 'forget' who we are. We forget where we're from, how we got here, what it is we're here to do, and how to begin to go about doing it.

Some theories would even go so far as to say that we choose our own

The only purpose of the soul is to grow; and growing means healing, healing means letting go and expanding.

parents, family and life-map, including the core growth and healing that we need to make in our own lifetimes. This is the concept of the soul's agenda, one that exists precisely in order that we can evolve, and grow. This theory is an elaboration, of course born from the human mind itself, of the basis on which creation, existence of matter, call it what you will, exists; that the universe is constantly expanding so all it can do is continue to expand. The metaphor around that in terms of human development is that our individual soul energy is incarnating or living a series of physical lives over and over

again in order to learn, grow and heal through numerous lifetimes. The only purpose of the soul is to grow; and growing means healing, because healing means letting go and expanding. Between each physical existence, we return to the quantum

creative soup, the divine origins of which we came from, having grown and carried back our new and expanded awareness.

SOULMATES

The people with whom we share our lives are, therefore, not an accident. Because at a deep level we are all connected, there is, in point of fact, no difference between any of us. However, as you go through life, you will find that there are certain people with whom you resonate more happily and easily than others. In energetic terms, these people comprise your soul group – other people with the same kind of vital spark of energy that you have; drops of water from the same part of the

The peace we need is always present, it's just that we have forgotten where it is and how to find it.

ocean, if you like. You know a soulmate when you meet one; you connect in ways that enable you to think and feel alike, your bodies may have similar characteristics and most outstandingly in humans, the eyes (that window of the soul) have a remarkably similar look to them. Animals, too, share soul groups with humans, and the energy of horses, dogs and dolphins is very close to our own. This could explain why you may even have a pet whose eyes closely resemble your own! Members of each soul group assist their fellow members along their individual personal journey here on earth (and on other energetic planes of existence). So, as you experience your own journey, you will meet others who encourage you, help you along the way, and with whom you will form lasting bonds.

PERFECT PEACE

How you perceive or think of your own deepest essence, how you see your own soul, is not particularly important. What is important is that you realise that this is the place within you where you are utterly perfect; where you are healthy, at peace, and happy. It's the place where healing is and where healing works. It's the place within you that has everything to do with finding your own healing not just momentarily, or for mopping up symptoms, but on a lifelong basis. So how can such a wellness within us ever allow us to become sick, or unhappy, or in crisis? Some spiritual teachers would say

that we experience what we have 'chosen' or 'need' to experience and that everything we live through is just one big lesson. I prefer to look at it another way: the peace we need is always present, it's just that we have forgotten where it is and how to find it; and our life experiences or conditioning have led us to build layers and layers of a defensive shell around us. We just don't remember how to be whole any more.

HEALING FROM YOUR SOUL

To understand the part that the soul plays in healing, and, more to the point, how we can actually get to touch that vital soul energy within, requires us to work backwards. First of all, it's your body that succumbs to physical illness, accident and disease. The immune system that protects your body from invasion by disease is affected whenever the mind is under stress. Whenever the mind says, 'whoa, hang on – we might have to

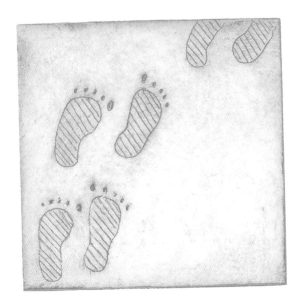

Clearly, it is important to ensure that your body is healthy in order to maintain immunity, general health, and wellbeing.

panic here!' it triggers the body to produce excess quantities of chemicals which effectively suppress our white blood cell production. White blood cells are responsible for managing immunity, so if they are suppressed from within, the body's

immunity is lowered, leaving it more open to invasion by disease and infection. Put simply, in a state of stress, the body becomes naturally weaker and vulnerable to all kinds of illness. So, the more you allow yourself to be in a stressful situation or to react in a stressed way to events around you, the more likely you are to become ill. Ironically, worrying about catching a cold from someone in your home or workplace will actually make you more likely to catch the cold!

Clearly, it is important to ensure that your body is healthy in order to maintain immunity, general health, and wellbeing. Eating good-quality, fresh food is vital. Food has an energy of its own, and the cleaner, fresher and less processed your diet is, the more you will benefit on levels other than

So, alongside good eating habits and gentle exercise routines, the first step to maintaining a healthy immune system is to find ways for your mind to function in a more relaxed way.

just the physical. There is a heightened awareness today of the effects of food. Wheat and dairy allergies are now recognised more and more frequently, as are intolerances to sugar and all manner of chemical additives in food and drink. As a rule of thumb, fresh and pure are best.

Gentle but regular physical exercise is also an essential part of maintaining physical and mental wellbeing. Once you make exercise a part of your daily life, you will find

that missing it leaves you feeling sluggish and uncomfortable. There are countless benefits to be gained from enjoying your body and building a level of basic fitness. You will boost your own self-esteem as your body firms up, and just raising basic muscle tone helps to counteract stress levels as posture and carriage begin to improve. This in turn helps to raise energy levels.

So, alongside good eating habits and gentle exercise routines, the first step to maintaining a healthy immune system is to find ways for your mind to function in a more relaxed way. Where does mental stress come from, and what can we do to combat it? Clearly, stress can be combated in ways ranging from learning to think more positively, to changing the colour and décor of your living space, to changing your activities and daily life and the people you spend your time with. But beating stress is not just a question of avoiding life; it's also about learning not to react with stress to situations that you find make you tense. So what is it that predisposes each of us to enjoy or not to enjoy, to become stressed or to feel relaxed by certain activities, colours, foods, places, and company? It is our basic energetic makeup – our innate needs and desires, our elementary character and calling that go to make up the aspect of the Self that we call the soul.

The traditional model of the soul would suggest that each of us is alive to fulfil a very specific purpose, and indeed, it is actually how we came into being. If you take a look at the story of creation, its essence is that God wanted to know what he was like – he wanted to know himself; so he sent bits of himself 'out there' so he could literally turn around and say,

Growth involves experiencing, releasing and then moving forward – what we would call healing.

'So that's what I'm like!' With nothing to provide a contrast or a mirror, he had no way of actually knowing what it was he was experiencing. Apply this metaphor to the more scientific theory of the unified field or quantum soup as God, the creative force, and you have a neat, potted explanation of how matter comes into existence; through the random but quite conscious shift from light waves to sub-atomic particles, and back again.

ENERGY – A BLUEPRINT FOR LIFE
The idea of the soul's need to become a real entity, to have a physical existence, appears not only throughout religious texts and classical spiritual literature, but also in the scientific world. Conscious energy needs a created, physical form through which to carry out the impulses it has to 'do' things and to experience its existence. So, matter comes into being; energy becomes a living, physical life. The soul is embodied. In the broadest sense of the soul agenda, the only purpose any of us has in being at all, is to grow. Growth involves experiencing, releasing and then moving forward – what we would call healing. Life, therefore, is a process of growth and healing, and all the events within your life, are there to provide opportunities for growth. As my mother would say when something appeared to be a total disaster – 'put it down to experience'.

Put simply, the concept of the soul agenda or basic soul makeup has a great deal to do with your physical and mental wellbeing. If you are, for example, a nature-lover who enjoys spending time outside, walking in the country, being around animals, and who is loving and nurturing, you are not going to thrive if you're cooped up in a modern office block in the middle of a town, with no facility to cater to your inner needs. Spending a long time within that environment would result in a degree of mental stress and the consequent physical knock-on effects in terms of illness, accidents and so on. Conversely, you may be a highly charged soul who loves to be around lots of people, noise and colour, who enjoys talking with others, being highly active and busy, hates the cold, wet and mud and

likes to be in a clean, bright environment. A walk in the country would probably be dull at best and a nightmare at worst. Working, say, on a farm, would be a recipe for misery, but a bright office in the city would probably have you on your toes and feeling good in no time. I have worked with dozens of clients who have come to me for healing and for help with their health and stress levels, who have benefited greatly from a change of job or a house move. I myself have been through that, having trained in accountancy when I left school, which was probably the most unsuitable career choice I could have made. Of course, I was miserable, depressed, took days off sick, constantly had colds, the flu,

What prompts us to embark on a spiritual journey is the knowledge that, at soul level, we're not comfortable.

and so on. Finally, I worked out that I hated being cooped up indoors all day every day, and bingo! The shift in my happiness was reflected in my overall vitality, and my mental and physical wellbeing improved, making stress and sickness a thing of the past. This is, of course, a simplistic example, and it is important to realise that who we are at an intrinsic energetic level is not identified by our role or career. Each of us is an individual and labels or roles are other people's way of relating to some aspect of us; often the only way to describe or explain ourselves is to say that 'we are'. But the point is that each of us has innate drives and desires, needs and dreams. Stifle that energy, and you suffocate the soul.

It would be simplest to say that sickness comes from a misalignment of the soul's agenda, which happens as a result of conditioned responses. What prompts us to embark on a spiritual journey, the search for something 'other', is very often the knowledge that, at soul level, we're not comfortable, hence the feeling of needing something, and the quest for whatever that may be. So if being well is just a matter of doing what makes us happy, surely it should be incredibly easy to heal ourselves? To a certain extent it is; but many people, when asked what they want to do with their lives, what it is that really drives them, and what they feel their own special purpose here is, have no idea. The aim then is to utilise the driving elements of your innate energy as part of your daily life, without identifying the things you do too strongly with who you really feel you are.

WHO AM I?

What activities do I most enjoy doing? When do I feel good about what I am doing – or what do I do that makes me feel I can really do this? What do other people tell me I am good at?

Is there anything I want to do or have always wanted to do that I'm not doing? Have I any unfulfilled ambitions or contributions I want to make to the world? Is there any opportunity I'm not taking up, or something that has been presented to me several times that I keep ignoring?

Is there a particular environment I enjoy? (e.g. being home alone or out socialising; staying in or going out. Do I prefer noise to quiet; or warm to cold? Would I rather be busy or inactive?)

Once you have answered the above questions honestly, compare your answers with the way you are currently living. This will give you an idea of any gap between where you are now, and where you need to be.

IN AN IDEAL WORLD

There are, on the other hand, many people who do have a very clear idea of how they would really like to spend their time in an ideal world, but who can see no way of making that a practical reality given the constraints of modern living. The biggest of those constraints, of course, is money and the practical need to provide for oneself. It's not always feasible for us to suddenly drop everything and run away to chant in a monastery in Tibet, though

CASE STUDY

LEONIE'S DEPRESSION

Leonie came to me suffering from depression. Although her depression lifted after using healing treatments, she always felt unhappy again by the time she came for her next appointment. It was clear that something in her life was simply not working for her. We talked and she explained that she was unhappy in her job, but just had no idea what she would rather do with her life. Leonie did not want to spend time on a daily basis in a pressurised, impersonal environment where the emphasis was just on profit. Her depression only really lifted long-term when she gave up work and found that actually, she didn't want a career at all but wanted to be a wife and mother — it was all about what she was actually doing with her life, about her unfulfilled need to nurture and create.

that might be what we feel we really need to do! I have a good friend who is a deeply spiritual soul and who wants nothing more than just to leave everything behind and live an uncomplicated, peaceful life — almost a monastic existence. With a husband, a mortgage that demands she works full-time and two teenage children, however, that's just not possible. So she contents herself with regular visits to a local Buddhist retreat. This kind of soul-weariness boils down to you making the changes you can within the scope you have for movement at any given time, and sticking with what feels right to you — with what it is within your integrity to do — all the way. Your own integrity is a natural warning system that helps to keep you from suffering inordinate levels of stress — it's as if there are degrees of discomfort with which you know you could genuinely not tolerate.

So, it's easy enough to say, 'Let's just not do what makes us unhappy!' In terms of career choice, where we live, how we spend our time and so on, that's perfectly possible. But it's also important to be aware that there are always going to be times when we just have to do things that we don't necessarily enjoy doing. This involves another aspect of healing yourself which is a deeper and far more powerful approach than just choosing to not do the things you don't like. That is not to suggest that you should participate in activities that you hate or are dangerous or damaging to you – that would not be following your integrity. But, learning to be more at ease and comfortable, instead of becoming stressed by life

Work on seeing life not as a restriction, but as an opportunity for fulfilment.

can be as simple as viewing the things that you might once have reacted to with stress, as no longer stressful. With the friend of mine mentioned above, I work on seeing life not as a restriction, or as ties that bind, but as an ongoing opportunity for fulfilment. She is working with the concept of mindfulness, or being present in the moment; so that she learns to see, for example, preparing food for her family, as being just as spiritually uplifting as meeting with her Buddhist friends. It's a question of perception, or perspective; of how we look at the events within our lives.

THE WAY OF THE WORLD

Perspective is something that is totally fluid; it's not something that is fixed, because it's within us. As the philosopher Nietzche would say, there is no such thing as the truth, there are only our own perceptions of it. If we think of each human soul as a little embodied fragment of the overall creative energy from which we came, it's easy to see ourselves as a miniature representation of the universe. Man can only be the microcosm of the macrocosm, because everything we see, understand and know, can only be seen, understood and known from our human perspective. An interesting example of that is people's implicit trust in 'science'; that it must be true, because it is the study of our world and how it works. That's all well and

good, but what we forget is that we can only see the world with tools that we create, and with the human eyes and brain with which we have to understand what it is we're studying. So basically, everything is open to interpretation purely because we are fallible; we are human. We make the tools, we look through the lenses, and we write down and interpret the

results of what we see. So each of us, and all that we understand about ourselves and the world around us, is purely the product of our own minds.

If you stop to reflect upon your own experience of the world you will see that there is, in fact, no such thing as 'good' or 'right' or 'true' — there are only different ways of seeing the world. For example, my mother has said that to listen to the

way each of her children describes their childhood, you would think we came from three different families. You will undoubtedly remember situations where you thought you were behaving in a certain way, and someone else — often the person closest to you — had an entirely different view of the situation. To take this concept a step further, consider a child, stomping around shouting, 'You hate me, don't you,' as a means of getting attention. We know perfectly well that we don't hate them, and they know it too, but

If you stop to reflect upon your own experience of the world you will see that there is, in fact, no such thing as 'good' or 'right' or 'true'.

what they want you to do is tell them you love them. In that moment, though they are loved, they are feeling hate. So whose is the correct, or truthful, view of the world? Is preparing the family dinner any less worthy or wonderful than chanting sanskrit mantras? Ultimately, everything we feel and think is totally subjective. What you think you see depends on how you look at it — is the glass half empty, or half full?

So how is it that we each learn to

see the world through such different eyes? We start our journey from a very physical place, as babies needing to be provided for. Then, as the psychologists would say, we begin to build defences due to our vulnerability and experience of our own needs. We build defences not only against the outside world, but against needs within ourselves, in learning to cope with being alive. We deal with what we feel inside; we deal with what we experience, and with that which other people present us. This is our conditioning, to build walls around ourselves so that we can function in the world. We work through a development of our needs, desires and awareness, to learning to form relationships with others, to providing for ourselves.

THE MEANING OF LIFE

Once we have all our walls in place, our needs catered for and we find ourselves with time to reflect, we then begin to ask – is that all there is? Is this it? Just providing? There must be a more meaningful experience of the world than this. What am I really here to be, and do? And here begins our personal spiritual journey. These days, with leisure time more available to us, and earning opportunities open to members of both genders and people of all ages, more of us are finding time to reflect. It used to be that people who came to learn about healing were middle-aged women whose husbands provided for them so that they had time on their hands and money in their pockets. Now, it's anyone who can provide for their own needs and still have some thinking time. So each of us lives a

Each of us lives a personal journey, which reflects man's journey through evolution.

personal journey, which reflects man's journey through evolution; from 'apes' experiencing an animalistic, needs-driven existence without consciousness, through an awakening of the mind and senses. Now, our evolution is seeing the development of the frontal lobes of our brains which is what allows us to process so much more information than ever before and to experience life on so many more levels than we have previously. It is this very process which is reflected within our search for the soul. So, as the soul-searching begins, we are now in a better position than ever before to fulfil that urge. And it's through our individual growth that evolution in the consciousness of humankind is taking place.

The so-called new era, or aquarian age, thus heralds the next phase of man's evolution. Much of this phase is involved in uncluttering and simplifying the way that we exist and experience our worlds. Raising our own awareness is a physical expression of the metaphor of bridging the gap between heaven and earth – of closing the gap between that peaceful state which is simplicity itself, and the existence we all muddle through as part of our daily lives. This state of being, to live our life in a fulfilled and healthy way is what each of us is aiming for. It's all a question of bringing your soul to the fore and aligning your essential self

To live our life in a fulfilled and healthy way is what each of us is aiming for.

or agenda with your physical life; of eliminating the 'rub' or friction between your deepest intent, and your reality.

In taking responsibility for your own healing, always remember that awareness-raising is not about 'improvement' or getting somewhere. Rather, it is about just being, watching, and living. Ultimately, by rising above the level at which you place great emphasis on what you're doing or where you are, you learn to transcend the level of 'stuff', and just Be. That's when you realise that cooking dinner and chanting are all the same thing. This is the

beginning of the state of enlightenment; it's a condition of gracious existence that has no aspect of conflict within it.

Man has evolved from an animal existence where we sensed, through having a thinking 'gap'. This is the gap that says, 'I can feel something, I know I can feel something. How do I make sense of this? Let me see. Let's analyse it….' Now, we're learning to silence that gap and simply be in the

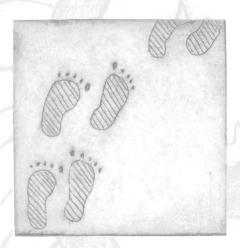

moment again, but in a new way. We are healing ourselves to a point of just being again, but this is not a downward transition. We've come full circle, only further on, so that we're actually learning to function from a state of awareness where we can understand what we experience and enjoy life instead of just plodding through it.

Some people would express this as being 'on flow' or 'in tune' with the way life is taking you, in order to live with the ultimate in peace and harmony and as little friction and stress as possible. So, in looking for ways to heal yourself, you will be finding ways to reach a state of deeper awareness, a higher consciousness and an entirely new perspective on your world. You will learn to look at your life through new eyes, to understand where you are, how you got there and where you're going. This, in turn, will benefit those around you as you provide the lead for others to follow, to learn from, and to begin their own journeys. Shifting your perception and raising your level of consciousness will enable the alignment of your own soul energy with physical life, for deep, lasting, stress-free, physical health and healing.

It is said that, as mankind becomes increasingly aware, everyone will be able to perceive different dimensions of life and energy; that Seeing, in the true sense of the word, is something all of us will do. How many people do you know who will openly confess 'Hey, I knew that was going to happen!', or who know who is on the telephone before they pick up the

Understand where you are, how you got there and where you're going.

receiver? The alignment of your soul energy with your physical existence means bringing about a total shift in consciousness to a point where things look very different. So, how do we do that? Every journey begins from where you are, so the first step in healing is understanding where that is, and working from there. In the next chapter, we'll look at ways to begin to understand your own energy system and how to heal it.

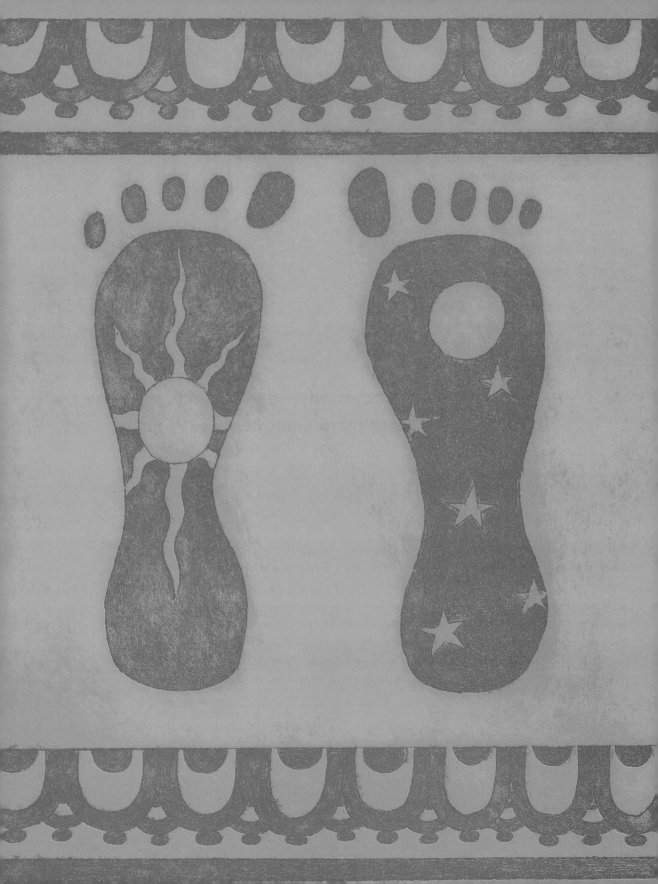

Starting your own healing begins with understanding where you are now; with the truth of your current situation. This does not necessarily mean going into a deep analysis of current problems and issues; sometimes, it can help if you understand how you arrived where you are. So, let's take a look at some of the factors that may have led you to the point at which you now find yourself. There are a few, very basic core problems that many of us suffer

CHAPTER 2

Appraisal

from, such as physical sickness (disease), and mental issues (e.g. depression, stress), and there are also some very simple answers to some of these, which is why you shouldn't need to do too much spadework.

Whatever your reason for seeking healing, blame should not come into the equation. Always remember that blame and judgement have no place here; this is one of the most important elements of any healing work that you undertake for yourself or other people. The mechanics behind holistic medicine, the mind-body school, have often been misunderstood and interpreted as a way of thinking which teaches us to see where one has 'gone wrong'.

We tend to start looking for the places where 'mistakes' have been made, or who or what in our lives may have had some bearing upon our current issues or situation.

The fact is, that wherever you are right now, is perfect for you, because it's the place from which you are going to find a way to shift whatever it is you need to shift. We rarely choose a path deliberately that we believe is going to mess up our lives. So, whatever it is that you're doing or have done to bring about the situation you're currently in, is probably the best that you could do

No matter how people appear to be behaving towards you, never forget that you have a choice.

at any given time, otherwise, you wouldn't have done what you did. Extend to others the possibility that they, too, might have been doing the best that they could do at any given time. Be aware that, whatever involvement anyone else has had in your life, has simply been an event in the past that has taken place. That's all it is. Those people would also have been doing whatever they thought was the right thing to do with their current knowledge, under the given circumstances. There may be a number of 'Yes, but's' popping into

your mind right now – instances of people who you feel have deliberately set out to annoy or hurt you, for example. We'll look at that a little more deeply elsewhere in this book, but for now, the premise that we're working from is that you take responsibility for your own life and your own healing.

CHOOSING DIFFERENTLY

As I mentioned in chapter one, my mother often refers to the fact that my sister, my brother and myself all describe certain childhood experiences very differently. Let's take a family outing for tea in a café as an example: I would describe it as a treat, and exciting; my sister might say that she didn't get the cakes she wanted so felt very upset; my brother might have noticed what the weather was like outside, or the fact that the café was busy so that we sat at two separate tables. The point is that in every given situation, the way that each individual sees it and how they feel about it, is down to them.

So, regardless of the events and experiences you have lived through or are living through in your life, and no matter how people appear to be behaving towards you, never forget that you have a choice. It is important to remember that your reactions, feelings, thoughts, responses and the way that you carry your experience with you, are entirely your own responsibility. Nobody else can decide how you feel, think or behave, or what you remember. Now, some of you may be saying, 'But I have had a terrible life. I was abandoned as a child, I spent my life in state care, I was assaulted as a teenager, I went

The world we see is entirely the result of our own perception; it's a mirror.

into a violent relationship, I ended up on the streets,' and so on. Some of you will say, 'I'm suffering a debilitating illness. How can I not be angry or depressed about that?' Again, it is always entirely your choice how you respond to a given situation.

There will always be times where you say, 'But hang on, that's just not real life.' In fact, it is. You can learn to think of a violent relationship as one in which you are treated badly, or one that gives you an opportunity to learn to love someone who is in very deep pain, and to love yourself enough to refuse violent treatment. You can choose to see a debilitating illness as a curse sent to wreck your life, or as an opportunity for a rest and an overhaul of your eating habits. The world we see is entirely the result of our own perception; it's a mirror. We can try to change

everyone or everything else, with all of the struggle and work that are part of anyone's mission to change the world. Or, instead, we can change the way that we look at things.

CREATING YOUR OWN REALITY
The first step is in learning to identify aspects of yourself and your life that you can begin to look at in a different way, and to heal. It is important to understand that there is nothing we manifest physically that hasn't first been an emotional event for us, whether it is physical sickness, emotional problems or life events. All the emotions we experience will, at some level, have created a physical reaction. Prior to that, a mental event will have taken place when you made a split-second response to what was happening in

CASE STUDY

JAKE

I worked on an ongoing basis with a young man named Jake who had been brought up in a violent and abusive home. He had been beaten for most of his life by both his mother and stepfather, given very little love or affection, and treated as a meal-ticket to earn money for the family by working hard from the age of four. Aside from the physical cruelty he endured, he was subject to all kinds of mental cruelty and abuse. His mother had four children by three different fathers (Jake never knew his own father) and blamed all of her problems and concerns on Jake. He was raped at the age of seven and never dared tell anyone.

At the age of twenty-five Jake was still being beaten and abused, forced to work eighteen-hour days, and was terrified of his mother's and stepfather's wrath to the point where they totally controlled his life. He was only allowed to socialise on their terms, and was kept financially dependent on his family. He was a poor communicator, deeply angry, and had grown up simply to repeat the patterns he had experienced: he became physically violent, he swung verbally between aggression and defence, he was argumentative, a compulsive liar, and was regularly in trouble with the police. He was also manipulative, and bad-tempered with animals to the point of beating and kicking them. He regularly got into physical fights with other people, both men and women, and had tried to kill his girlfriend on a number of occasions, causing her all kinds of injuries. He suffered from chronic back pain, irritable bowel syndrome, and pains in all of his joints, particularly his knees, hips, and ankles.

When Jake came to see me, I saw a very handsome, imaginative, talented, and caring young man who was clearly deeply disturbed. As his story unfolded, it would have been easy for me to see him as someone I would rather have had locked up, than helped; my own exercise in changing my perception was to continue to see the purity in him behind the mess he presented. Over time, Jake began to heal simply by learning to see that the life he had been given at home, in particular by his mother, was all she knew how to give him. Had she been capable of treating him any differently, she would have done so. He learned to see his mother as the product of another abusive family, as someone who was as wounded, fearful, and angry as he was, but who had never learned to let go of her anger.

Jake made the decision to sit down for five minutes twice a day and remember the pain of his life, but to look at it with understanding and a total shift of perception in order to try to acknowledge the reasons why his mother had done what she did. Eventually, over the course of many years, Jake did let go of much of his anger and fear and learned to relate to his parents simply as people. He gained the courage to leave their control and live a life of his own, and gradually his health improved as he physically let go of the emotional patterns of stress that he had been holding for so long. By learning to shift his perception of his own life story, he totally changed his existence.

your environment. First, you perceive, think and understand something. Then, you may have a reaction to that. Then, you'll make a decision as to what to do with that reaction and how you are going to carry that experience with you. It is vital always to remember that, because at a deep level all matter is inter-connected, whatever you choose to call into being is very likely to occur. So, on that basis, you can choose the events that you bring into your own life.

I'll give you an example. A woman came to me for healing following a traumatic and messy relationship breakdown. She talked me through the history of her last three relationships. The first was with someone whom she found out was two-timing her with another woman. She also mentioned that he was verbally, and occasionally physically, abusive. So, she told him to leave, and, after much fighting, the relationship finished. Then, she married a man who later turned out to have been having an affair throughout their married life and who, when challenged, became violent and aggressive towards her. So, they split up. Finally and most recently, she married a man who appeared to be gentle, kind, faithful, and deeply caring. However, as she told me herself, she found it impossible to trust his motives, and was utterly convinced that everything would fall to pieces in due course.

Because she found herself unable to trust him, she would telephone him constantly on his mobile phone whenever he left the house. In spite of his making every effort to comfort and reassure her, she became more and more fearful. She would telephone him more and more frequently, even during working hours, and convinced herself that he must be having a relationship with another woman, if not at any other time, then certainly during office hours! Her husband found he had to turn off his telephone or not take his wife's calls as it became impossible to concentrate on work or to attend necessary meetings for any length of time. Naturally, on finding his telephone turned off, his wife grew even more suspicious, and would fly into a rage the moment he arrived home. In response, he

Every one of us has the power to create in our lives whatever it is that we choose to experience.

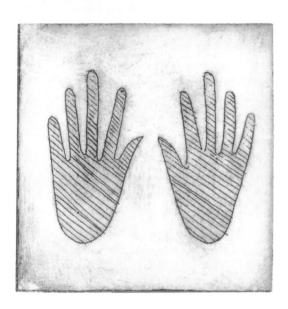

would come home later and later to avoid spending time in such an angry atmosphere. Eventually, he did become involved with another woman at which point his wife came to me, saying, 'You see! They are all the same! I said he would leave me and he has! There is no such thing as a faithful man.'

What this woman failed to recognise was that she was the common denominator; that in fact she had chosen all three of these men to be a significant part of her life. The first two were, in fact, almost the same 'type' of individual, and her attraction to them was a result of her own low self-image and feelings of unworthiness. Finally, she chose to be with a partner who really did love her, and who was utterly dependable, but instead of breathing a sigh of relief, she chose to recreate her previous two relationships. She called into being the reality with which she was most familiar, and that which she expected to happen, by creating the ideal circumstances for it to become fact.

LETTING GO

This example I have just given is a very sad one, but one that I have seen the like of many times before, and one with which, I'm sure, we can all identify on some level. Most of us have been in or are still caught in cyclic patterns of behaviour within which we recreate our own disasters. It might be something as simple as 'forgetting' to pay the bills on time, or not leaving enough time to make a journey so that you always arrive late, or not taking care of your health so that you succumb to illness. At the same time, we are all capable of creating positive, prosperous, and happy events in our own lives by making a decision to choose the outcome that we desire, whether it be to earn a given salary, to live in a certain house, to have a child, or to spend a day in a particular place in a way that we choose to do. Each and every one of us has the power to create in our own lives whatever it is that we choose to experience. So, going back to taking responsibility for your own healing, let's say that where you are now is the right place for you; it's the place from which you can choose to be and do whatever it is that you choose to be and do. The world really is your oyster!

From where you are right now it may not look as though you hold the world in your hands. Sometimes it seems as though there is no further down that we can go, that there is no possible way out. But when you reach that place, all you need to be aware of is one thing – that every challenge is an opportunity for change. Every situation in which you find yourself is a chance for you to find ways to make a difference within you own life, and the way to begin that is to understand the pattern that created your current situation.

The easiest way to trace the origins of your current situation, whatever it is, is just to stand back and look at your life from the point of view of an outsider. Look at your situation, present and past, as if it were someone else's. Developing this detached view of yourself and your own circumstances is a tool that can help you throughout your healing process, as well as more generally in your everyday life. If you are able to maintain a detached perspective during what could potentially become emotionally charged circumstances, you will begin to see the value in just taking a step back and observing for a moment before taking any action. Snap decisions or judgements are often based purely on an emotional

Look at your situation, present and past, as if it were someone else's.

response, and are not always helpful or beneficial to you. Of course, having made a decision, you will learn whether or not you would want to repeat that experience. Sometimes you would; and other times, it would help you not to react the same way in future.

You might feel that if you work from a detached viewpoint it means you're emotionally cold or hard, but this isn't the case. It can be a far more loving and helpful way to work with other people and their issues than if you were to invest your own emotions in their problems. For example, remaining detached from the panic and shock in an accident

DEVELOPING A DETACHED VIEW

Realise that your own view is just one view. There are countless other ways of seeing yourself and your own situation.

At any given moment during the day, stop what you are doing and ask yourself: Am I doing this because it makes me happy? Do I feel at peace? If not, how do you feel? Are you sad, worried, angry, tense?

Ask yourself why you are doing what you are doing. Is it to please someone else? Is it because you feel pressurised by another person? Is it out of fear? Or does it stem from a need to control? If what you are doing is not fulfilling, change it.

Before you embark on a new task, journey, or interaction during your day, stop for a moment and ask yourself: Do I feel at peace? If you have any rumblings of discomfort in your gut, you can guarantee that is a sure sign that you are not totally happy with what you are doing. Another good question to ask is, Am I doing this because I want to, or because I must? This can begin to show up your habitual behaviour, too.

After you have completed a task, journey, or interaction with another person, ask yourself, 'Did that enrich me? Then ask yourself: Did it enrich them? Remember this is not about self-sacrifice; it's about staying with your integrity. If you weren't enriched by the experience, what would you do differently next time? How would you have behaved in a more enriching way to the other people involved? Remember, that can mean saying no, as well as yes. Do you actually need to do anything?

As you find yourself talking to another person or doing something during your day, imagine standing outside yourself as an observer, a third person. Ask yourself, do I look happy? If you feel any discomfort, stop and ask yourself where the discomfort is coming from.

The oldest and most effective question to ask yourself periodically during the day is: If I were compelled to repeat this moment for ever, would I be happy to do it?

situation enables you to function far more effectively, usefully, and practically than those who are busy engaging in the fear and trauma, becoming panicked or fearful themselves. Having worked alongside those who are medically trained in emergency situations, I have witnessed for myself their calm demeanour during a crisis, and how that simple detachment has a calming effect on the people around them. The same principle applies when interacting with someone who has a serious illness or is undergoing some kind of life crisis. Of course, you can empathise with that individual, but by allowing yourself to become caught up in the emotion of the moment, you may take on so much of their trauma as to be no longer useful to them.

UNCONDITIONAL BEING

Detached view is also the basis of unconditionality, another key principle in healing you and other people. It's a concept that relates to my earlier points about blame, judgement, and responsibility for your own life. An unconditional viewpoint is one from which you do not judge, you do not blame, and above all, you maintain a peaceful and caring attitude, in spite of what others say or do around you.

Unconditionality is one of the most useful keys you could ever have

Your anger is an outward projection of your inner feelings.

to healing yourself. Instead of deciding to react with anger, offence or fear to what others say and do to you, you can decide to maintain your peace. This sounds like a tall order, but in fact if you detach, and think of others as doing what you might do in any given situation, a state of calm is not difficult to achieve.

For example, when you are shouting or snapping at someone else, it is likely to be because you are feeling upset, tired, or hurt. Your anger is an outward projection of your inner feelings. Going back to the example I gave in chapter one, of the child who shouts 'I hate you', it's rarely the case that the child truly hates their parent; it might just be that he or she is being thwarted in their own desires and feels angry about that. So, a useful way to help you learn to develop a detached view is to try seeing those around you as children. All the noise, shouting, verbal abuse, foul behaviour, or anger, is an outward projection of frustration and hurt. True, some people are like that a lot of the time, and they are probably holding on to a very old and longstanding hurt, or they feel constantly re-hurt or angry because they perceive things as being 'out to get them'. They are working on memory, living in the past, instead of going with what's currently

See your life as a series of interrelated events that have led you to where you are now.

happening. So, stop and ask yourself – in what situations am I living in the past? Where am I judging by experience instead of facing each new situation without preconceptions?

Observing your life from a detached viewpoint is also a step towards understanding the significance of certain events as part of your life's path. This might include the place where you lived as a child, the school you went to, the people you met at college, a contact you made at your first job, the way you

met your partner, how you came to be living in your current home, and so on. Practise seeing your life in a detached way; as a series of interrelated events that have led you to where you are now. Then, you might start to see a pattern emerging that you can understand and use to find a way forward, or perhaps even see where the culmination of your life's events have been leading you to. This is what Jung called synchronicity; a series or chain of events that seem coincidental but which in fact have an eerie kind of harmony to them. This is the way of the universe; because of the intrinsic interconnection throughout all life. What you need to come to you will come, and will be perfect in its timing and manner of arrival.

The lady with the series of broken relationships could see absolutely no way forward from her current situation; she was tired of finding a new life, pinning all her hopes upon it, then 'watching everything fall to pieces' around her. But in talking through the situation, she realised that had this been the life of one of her friends. She would have suggested they choose a more honest and gentler kind of man than the first two, as a life partner. Having found that man, she would have told them to do everything they could to learn to trust him instead of nagging and panicking. She would have suggested that they learn to be more honest, and to talk about their issues, asking their partner for support instead of attacking him. And so, my client has come to realise that, though she would never have wished for her second marriage to fail, it happened for a reason, so that she could finally sit back, take a deep breath, and get some help with her problems, instead of going through the same cycle one more time. Instead of creating the reality that she expects to experience, she can now make a decision to choose and expect to have a new experience, and she can create that as her new reality. This is how the energy field that is the universe works.

TRUSTING THE PROCESS

Having established how you got to where you are, remember that nothing has been an accident, because it has all led you to the place from which you are starting your healing process. Some of the processes you have gone through in order to get here might seem bizarre, because you do not always get what you want in the way you think you want to receive it – but you will always get what you need! Sometimes we might say, 'But I needed a new car,' or 'I really needed that job,' or, 'I didn't need that dose of flu!', but the point is, there was a level of your being (often deeply

unconscious) at which you desired to create those experiences, otherwise you would not have experienced

Make a decision to choose and expect to have a new experience.

them. So, instead of seeing what appear to be challenging situations as a stumbling block or obstacle, learn to view them as an opportunity to make a change, to shift things, or to let go of circumstances. This is exactly what my client with the string of unhappy relationships is learning about her own life. Sometimes the very experiences, memories or emotions that you feel you could never let go of, are the very things that you really need to shift. That principle might even extend to your job, your home, or the person you share your life with. It is always true that if you let go, something much better comes along. So-called life crises, challenges, illness, and apparent unhappiness are not just things that are sent to try us. They

are valid opportunities for making changes, to see what life is showing us and to move forward in a new, exciting, and different way. Within every situation, there is always an opportunity for healing and growth.

You can see this phenomenon all around you in the lives of other people, if you take the time to look. I have worked with so many clients who, having been diagnosed with chronic or terminal illness have used that death-threat as an opportunity to learn to live every single moment. The first person who ever came to

me for healing having been given only a short time to live said to me, 'I only have six months!' and wept as I held her hands. I responded with the only words that came into my head, which were, 'Well – did you know how long you had to live before?' She looked up at me, paused a moment, then threw her head back and roared with laughter. 'You know,' she said, 'I had never thought of life like that. I have always taken so much for granted!' And as we laughed together, she added, 'You could even die before me!', to which I replied, 'The point is, Helen, that any one of us could die at any moment. That's a very good reason to really LIVE!'

SEIZING THE DAY

There is something of the Buddhist in this approach – the attitude that says why hit yourself over the head with tomorrow, when you could be truly, deeply living each and every moment? It's this idea of *carpe diem* (seize the day) that brings life into sharp focus with all of its colour, vibrancy and joy and enables you to really live. Helen was someone I will always deeply admire; from the moment of our talk, she made a decision to live her life utterly and completely. In fact, she outlived her medical prognosis by several years, and lived more in those few years than, as she so often put it, 'I have lived in my entire life'. After all, life is so very precious; why spend it standing around waiting for something to happen, or hoping that someone else will fix it? It's about taking responsibility and living every day as if it were your last.

Helen provides a beautiful example of how what has become known as 'the dark night of the soul' can actually be that darkest moment before the true light of dawn and the beginning of a very deep healing process. Each of us goes through this experience at some point in our life. It's a time of bleakness, desolation and utter despair, when every last thing seems to have gone wrong, and there is absolutely no way that you can see a light at the end of the tunnel. It is also a time when people make significant changes in their lives for the better. Some people find spirituality, some change their eating habits, others take up a new sport or hobby, while others leave their jobs and go back to college, some travel the world, and some people retire. It all depends on what it is each of us most needs to do to express ourselves in a joyful, peaceful way at that given moment. But you can guarantee that the crisis, sickness or other disaster in your life has taken place as a means of bringing about a necessary shift.

I recently held a workshop at which two of the people attending had both suffered major accidents; both had broken their backs, and lived through the resultant debilitation and pain, which is what led them to learn about healing and holistic health. Through their own experiences and learning, they have both gone on to become therapists

> *The point is to learn to see the signs and to 'go with the flow', before the crises or sickness happens, and that's what I hope to help you do.*

who help heal the lives of numerous other people and animals.

DARKEST BEFORE DAWN

Without exception, each of the people I have worked with who has lived through that dark night of the soul and come through the other side, has valued that process as a time of significant growth and healing. The point is to learn to see the signs and to 'go with the flow', before the crises or sickness happens, and that's partly what I hope to help you to do through this book. We'll look in more detail at how to maintain your awareness at a level that will allow you to learn to move with the flow of energy in your life in chapters six and seven. It doesn't matter that you may not have been living that way until now. Some healers or spiritual teachers might say that by ignoring your soul's needs for so long, you did the wrong thing which is why you came to the point where you experienced the crisis. I, however, take the view that purely by experiencing whatever it is that has led you to the point of wanting to heal your soul, you are in the perfect situation for you.

HARNESS YOUR INTENT

So, let's harness your intent to find your way out of the situation you're in now, and get moving. Intent, it has to be said, is vital in all forms of healing, because you will bring into your life whatever you think or wish for. You are creating your own reality purely through the consciousness of interconnected energy at each and every moment. It is therefore important to enter any healing

Once you place that intent into your own healing, your world will start to move and change for the better.

process or journey with the intent that, no matter what, you will keep going until you feel at peace and free from all your past anxieties. Once you place that intent into your own healing, your world will start to move and change for the better almost from the moment you begin.

I have found that it can help to actually focus the energy of your intent upon your own healing process, and on what your desired aim or healed outcome will be.

Let's go back to the example of my client with the three broken relationships (see p. 41). First of all, she focused her intent on changing her situation: on learning to have a lasting, happy relationship. She took a step back and from her detached view, looked at her situation. How did she get there? She got there by entering relationships with two men who, she is well aware, she chose because they were the kind of men that women always wanted to be with. They were good-looking, rogueish, and available. My client felt that because they showed her some attention, they must be 'the one'. However, once she was in a relationship with each of those men, she always felt a sense of insecurity and thought that they might just as easily leave her for other women, because deep down she knew this was their pattern. She freely admits that when the third man came along she almost forced him into a corner in terms of how the relationship broke down, because she could not understand how to live her life any other way.

So, how could she do things differently in future? What would her healed outcome be? In this case, she decided that she truly did love her second husband. She realised that he was a good man and that, if at all

HARNESS YOUR INTENT

1 Sit down in a quiet space where you know you will be undisturbed.

2 Take a pen and paper and write at the top of the sheet the issue you are currently facing, or the pattern you want to change. For example, it might be: I have to have another operation; or I argued with my wife again; or it could be I ate ten bars of chocolate and I wasn't even hungry. There may be a whole list.

3 Realise that the reason this pattern occurs in your life is because you are creating it.

4 Now, below the issue write down: I create my own reality. This is the point at which you can feel the shift beginning to occur. Just as you created your own pattern, you have the ability to create a new one. So, think about your healed outcome; what would you like to do differently. Write that down next. It might be: I can choose to be healthy; or, I can create a harmonious relationship.

5 Sit for a moment and realise what this actually means. You are placing your intent into a whole new cycle of being; a whole new way of experiencing your life.

6 Now let your mind drift and imagine all kinds of positive scenarios that could replace the one you have been in. See yourself in a different home, place, or time – on the moon, on a beach, skiing, sitting in a chair reading a book, and so on. See yourself experiencing peace and happiness. Then realise that this is how you can feel, from this moment onwards, and on an ongoing basis. Always remember that the specifics of how your situation changes are not necessarily going to be what you expected. But if you place your energy behind living your life in a different way and creating the changes you need to create, you can rest assured that they will take place.

7 Finally, keep your sheet of paper with you, and whenever you remember to, take it out and read what you have written. Over a period of time you will begin to see that the reality you were in when you wrote those words is quite a different one from the one you are in now.

possible, instead of learning to live in a trusting way in a new relationship, she would dearly love to have the opportunity to trust him and be with him again. Of course, that will involve a radical shift in her behaviour, her husband's willing support, and a big leap of faith on both parts. She also has to learn not to place blame on the men in her

life, to take responsibility for her own part in the scenario, and to learn to see that what she sees is largely a projection of her own pain. In other words, she created her own reality, because all the while she was seeing her husband as untrustworthy, she was simply expressing her own inability to trust. She also has to learn that she can just as quickly create a new reality.

So, you can see that projection is a powerful emotional tool and one that is behind so many of our difficulties in relating to other people. However, remember that healing is not about blaming the person in your life and using them as the mirror on to which you project your pain. Neither is it about blaming yourself for feeling what you felt, or what you did, or the way that you did it. Projection should be used to create healing in your life just as easily as you do pain, just by projecting yourself differently.

I have cited an example of emotional healing, but the same principles apply to cases of physical illness, too. The physical sickness that we experience is our body's way of waving a flag; of bringing us to the point where we realise that we must learn to do things differently. Helen ignored all her early warnings, and decided not to bother to change her diet, stop drinking, or living in ways that created a great deal of mental stress, so she was effectively setting her body up for sickness. It's simple enough to see the signs when your body says, 'Look! I can't handle this!' and to make some simple changes in your life for the better, in order to help to promote your own healing. Even the very parts of our body that exhibit physical dis-ease are giving us a clue about what it is that we're doing emotionally that we need to heal and change! Louise Hay's classic self-healing book, *You Can Heal Your Life* has a wonderful list showing how the parts of the body that manifest dis-ease relate to our emotional processes. For example, knees are about flexibility, so knee problems tend to occur at times when we are working from an inflexible stance. Our back is the structure that supports us, so back pain tends to occur as a result of feeling unsupported; either emotionally, spiritually, or even financially. So whenever you find that your body is waving a flag at you, don't just panic and reach for the pills – treat it as an opportunity for change.

HEALING NOW

Here are some straightforward, practical exercises to help you shift your view of situations, and help you change your perception of where you are now, how you got here, and where you're going to go next. You can add your own examples to the two columns shown below:

PAST SITUATION	INSTEAD OF THIS I COULD SEE
I had a terrible childhood	*My family did all they knew how to do*
My marriage failed	*We worked at it as best we could at the time*
I lost my job	*That was how I got to where I am now*
I had a terrible sickness	*If I hadn't been ill, I would never have taken up golf*

CURRENT SITUATION	INSTEAD OF THIS I COULD SEE
Someone in my life offended me	*I don't need to be offended, I can choose to let it go*
Someone made me angry	*The anger is mine; I can choose peace*
I'm running out of money again	*This is an opportunity to earn/save money in a different way*
My relationship is falling to pieces	*This is the time to do something radical to make a change for the better*
I have a debilitating illness	*It's time to take care of myself a little more*

By now you will have identified what it is about your current pattern and way of being that you would like to release. So, having placed your energetic intent with the aim of your own healing for long-term growth, it's now time to take a look at some ways in which you can begin to understand and work with the healing process.

CHAPTER 3

Awareness

YOUR ENERGY BODY

In order to understand how we live and experience our lives, let's first examine what we are as human beings in terms of energy. The physical body that we have is, in energetic terms, the expression of a conscious energetic desire to have an experience. It is the means with which to 'be' and 'do'. In the first chapter, I explained that all matter has at its essence a conscious, living energy that has an innate drive for action. The creation and existence of a physical body is therefore just the way in which the living energy finds a means with which to carry out its drive for action. Thus, your physical body is not there only, as some healers might say, to house your soul!

Your body is to be honoured because it is vitally important in terms of your soul agenda and overall healing; without it, your innate drive and desire have no means with which to express and fulfil themselves. So the physical body is, in fact, the final expression of a fourth-dimensional energetic existence. Your energy field or energy 'body' has several densities, sometimes called 'layers', which surround your physical body. The expression of these densities of energy as layers is the easiest way for our finite minds to understand an infinite concept. The energy field surrounding us is composed of ever-finer energy, of ever higher vibrational frequency, that is at its deepest level the basic energy with which we are all interconnected – the energy that is light. For this reason, you will sometimes hear your energy body described as your light body; another word for it is the aura.

As the 'layers' or distinguishable

bands of energy within your energy field become gradually higher in frequency and so less dense and physical, the frequencies within which your energy functions move beyond the normal perception of our physical human senses. Most people can see and feel the closest or densest layer of the energy body, which is known as the etheric layer. This is a protective, energetic 'space-suit' for your physical body, and is what people sometimes perceive as 'hanging around' after someone dies. (Incidentally, most energicians – people who work with energy – would not describe the death of the physical body as the end of life, but as a shift in the dimensional levels of our existence, or a change in the level of consciousness with which we experience our existence).

TO SEE ETHERIC ENERGY

Ask someone to stand or sit in front of a plain-coloured wall; it helps if the light is slightly down. Do not concentrate or squint, just direct your focus to the person's face, and see if you become aware in your peripheral vision of a blue-white layer surrounding the body. It will look like a gentle glow around the person you are observing, almost as if it is 'on' the wall behind them. This is the energy that is often represented as a halo around the heads of spiritual figures in ancient texts.

You can also feel this energy with your hands. First rub your hands together for a moment to sensitise them, then extending your arms in front of you, gradually bring your hands slowly towards each other, or towards the surface of another person's body. You usually register the feeling of the 'cushion' or magnetic sense of the etheric energy first in your fingertips. Then, it will spread to your palms as you focus your awareness on it.

Experiment a little with distance from the body's surface; the etheric energy can be felt anywhere from a couple of inches off the surface of the skin up to seven or eight inches away. Most usually it is around three or four inches away from the physical body.

The next density or layer is the emotional energy or 'astral' energy, which has a band of lower-frequency, and a band of higher-frequency energy. It is at this point that the energy body begins to have a presence in what scientists would call other 'dimensions'. I will cover this in more detail in the chapter on reaching your soul energy, but for the time being, remember that you are, at any given moment, a multi-dimensional being capable of shifting

Energy field damage can take place through the way that you internalise a memory or event.

your awareness to other aspects of space and time.

Outside or beyond the emotional energy is your mental energy, which also has two frequencies; the concrete mental energy, where we understand thoughts and concepts; and the abstract mental energy, where thoughts and perceptions occur in a random way. This is the energy that we seek to reach and shift our awareness to during meditation. We are aiming to move past all the emotional turmoil, and past all the thoughts and chatter of our everyday mental awareness. It is with our awareness in this dimension or frequency that we can begin to find the answers to issues that we're

currently facing; but more on this in the section on meditation later on. A still higher frequency of energy is beyond or above that of our mental energy, which is that of the soul or spiritual level energy. Beyond this is the level at which we are all, quite simply, connected with one energetic frequency – the creative source from which we all originate. Your energy field extends for many feet in diameter around your physical body. Often people who draw the human energy field will draw a shell or line around it – but there is no edge, there is a level at which it cannot be perceived even by those deeply sensitive individuals who can see or otherwise perceive the aura.

BLOCKING THE FLOW

It is within your energy body that disturbances and impediments of flow occur first. As I explained in chapter one, if your soul energy is constantly stifled or misdirected, then all the other aspects of your energy body will become disturbed, affecting mental stress levels, emotional wellbeing, and physical health. Disturbances can occur anywhere within your energy body. They may take place, for example, as a result of the way you process the words that someone else speaks to you, to create a thought-form that is detrimental to your overall wellbeing. Energy field damage can also take

BIOLOGY STUDENT

I recently came across a biology student who, having learned about the cardiovascular system became morbidly fascinated with the workings of the human heart. His lecturer had told the class that the human heart was 'born with a capacity for a finite number of beats; and nothing you can do will change that'. Our student became convinced that as a fitness fanatic, all the running and aerobic exercise he had done had actually shortened his life! So he stopped exercising, and adopted habits that meant he exerted himself as little as possible. Over time, the more he energised it and dwelt upon it, the thought-form that his heart was a liability became quite entrenched in his energy. He came to me when he had almost become frightened of the process of being alive. He shifted this energetic disturbance within his own field quite simply with some energy healing treatments that worked directly upon his energy field. Then, in time, as his energy became a little more free and less entrenched in its pattern, he was able to create some new thinking patterns and thus influence his physical activity.

place through the way that you internalise a memory or event; it may have been quite harmless, but one that you have 'filed' in a certain way that has become detrimental to your own process.

Once a disturbance or blockage exists within your energy, the effects will be felt throughout your energy body. If you're labouring under an energetic disturbance, you might continue to live with that aspect of yourself and not actually look at your own process. If you don't change anything physically or address the issue, your emotional level energy can also become affected and your emotions begin to manifest in a distorted or disturbed way. We all

If you don't address the issue, your emotional level energy can be affected.

know how easy it is to get snappy when we're worried about something, but there are also those of us who habitually worry about the same things. Eventually, the effect of the compounded energetic disturbance throughout your mental and emotional energy will become apparent at a physical level; usually in the lower back. Your physical body, as the ultimate expression of your energetic essence, has finally become compromised. This is why symptoms of ill-health can be seen as a kind of flag-waving. It's the body telling you that there's something you really need to address, because the protective and sustaining life-force energy that expresses itself as your physical body, is just not functioning clearly and fluidly. If it were, you would be in perfect physical health.

UNDERSTANDING YOUR CHAKRAS

The primary energy 'system' that can be used to help with healing is the chakra system. The use of energy tools to help shift the current state of being, or, put more simply, energy medicine (which includes aromatherapy, reflexology, acupuncture/pressure, flower remedies, crystals, colour and sound therapy, among others), can be understood without difficulty and worked with by beginners. For those more used to working with energy, it's possible to go into great depth about the therapeutic ways in which we can work with our chakras. Chakra is a derivation of the sanskrit word for 'wheel', and is the name given to the spinning vortices of energy that surround the human body and exist within the energy field. The chakras form part of the energy body and can almost be thought of as a sensory system that emanates energy from the physical end energetic body, and draws in energy from the greater energy source surrounding us.

Chakras are often described as being like flowers, having stems and petals. I, however, perceive them as a reinforced and more active section of the energy field; almost as if those are the 'clumps' of energy within the human field that we have repeatedly used during our experiences of living. For me it's almost as if constantly using those energetic frequencies strengthens them to the point where they appear more robust and active than the rest of the energy 'cocoon' which surrounds the physical body. This energetic strengthening can be likened to the way in which constantly exercising a part of your physical body – one leg, say – would result in a tougher, stronger and better defined muscular structure in that area. The chakras emanate from the physical body in the same way as the energy field does, and though they can be felt primarily at the front and back of the body, they are flexible and mobile and you can actually feel them to a degree all around the physical body.

Generally, in terms of healing, the descriptions of function and energetic frequencies involved with each chakra are limited to the seven major chakras. There are, in fact hundreds of them, including the tiny mini-chakras that exist at the junctions of the physical energy pathways (meridians) that are utilised in therapies such as reflexology, acupuncture and acupressure. The reason why therapists have concentrated on seven main chakras for years seems to be that these are the ones that have always been most important to our human experience and healing. More recently, people have begun to notice other chakras 'appearing' and to investigate how these chakras are involved in our energetic development. I feel that as we develop and grow as human beings, and our brains, consciousness and awareness undergo some radical shifts, we are simply beginning to 'exercise' and strengthen new parts of our energy field, giving the impression of a 'new' chakra.

THE CHANGING CHAKRA SYSTEM

The reason why I perceive the chakras and their development in this way is because, through my work with animals of all species, I have seen a whole variety of different forms of energy field and chakras. I have found that generally, a very simple species such as, say, a worm, has a far less complex energy system than that of, say, a horse or dolphin.

There are hundreds of chakras that exist at the junctions of the physical and energy pathways.

The number and strength of the chakras you can perceive within the energy fields of different animals varies according to that species' use of different aspects of its energy field. I do also perceive a difference in the complexity and strength of chakras within the energy fields of babies and adults. Of course there are also variations between adults who tend to focus their energy more on certain chakras than others, and those who are undergoing shifts in their own use of energy.

The main chakras can be found down the centre line of the body, and they correspond physically to points on the endocrine system. A great deal is known about the seven main chakras as far as their role in our energetic, mental, emotional and physical health is concerned; somewhat less is known about the others. It is worth mentioning here two other chakras. The first is usually known as 'alter major' (the nose/mouth chakra). It is involved in the energetic experiences that many of us are going through at the moment, particularly in terms of consciousness-raising and bridging the gap between higher level energies and our physical existence. Not a great deal of work is currently done with this chakra but I suspect that it will become more prominent in healing work very soon. The second 'new' chakra is one that a teacher of mine has called the meta-heart, as it is between the heart and throat. This chakra is also becoming more active and present in the human experience, as it is related to energies involved in finding our spiritual truth.

For the sake of understanding ways in which you can help to release energetic patterns and shift your

energy to allow healing to take place, I am going to focus on the role of the main chakras within the energy field. (There are various other recognised energy systems within the human energy field.) Because the chakras do correspond to parts of the endocrine system and the physical body, imbalances within a particular chakra are likely to create physical

The old theory that one could 'open' or 'close' chakras is just not true.

symptoms related to that area of the body and endocrine system.

People tend to think of the chakras as being 'attached' to the body, and although this is the way they are expressed in pictorial form, they aren't actually located in specific physical places. Because the chakra energies extend in so many directions and at different vibratory frequencies, the entire energy system is truly multi-dimensional. So, you need not worry too much about exactly where to find them, because they will shift to meet the energy you're working with. This is where it is important to recognise the role of intent, as an expression of the conscious living energy that is your own essence. For example, if you decide you want to feel someone's heart chakra energy but place your

CHAKRA	ASSOCIATED ENDOCRINE
Crown	Pineal
Third Eye	Pituitary
Throat	Thyroid
Heart	Thymus
Solar Plexus	Islets of langerhans
Sacral	Adrenals
Base or Root	Gonads

hand near their feet, you will begin to perceive the energy of the heart, because your intent will focus on heart energy and the heart energy will respond to that intent.

I should also mention at this point that the old theory that one could 'open' or 'close' chakras is just not true. If you could somehow close your chakras, the lack of energetic interaction between your body and the energy source that you need to sustain your existence would not take place. Your energy levels could not be sustained and so neither could your physical existence. The only time that the chakras steadily begin to close down is as we die. Chakras can, however, become unbalanced, distorted, blocked, and either over- or underactive. When this happens, the disruption within your energy field is likely to affect so much of your energy body that there will undoubtedly be mental, physical, and emotional symptoms related to the particular band of frequencies where the disruption is. The chakra or chakras concerned will either be the focus of an excess of energy, or a deficiency.

ENERGY IMBALANCES

It may be that you suffer from an occasional imbalance in one or more chakras, or that you habitually function with your energies excessively through a particular

CHAKRA	ASSOCIATED ORGANS
Crown	Skin, muscular system, skeletal system
Third Eye	Brain, nervous system, eyes, ears, nose
Throat	Throat, trachea, mouth, teeth and gums, oesophagus
Heart	Heart, circulation, lungs, shoulders and arms, ribs, breasts, diaphragm
Solar Plexus	Abdomen, stomach, upper intestines, liver, gallbladder, kidneys, pancreas, adrenals, spleen
Sacral	Adrenals, large intestine, pelvis, appendix, bladder, hips
Base or Root	Genitals, legs, bones, feet, rectum, immunity

CHAKRA	ASSOCIATED SICKNESS
Crown	Energetic disorders, sensitivity to stimuli
Third Eye	Brain tumour, stroke, neurological, blindness, deafness, fitting
Throat	Throat, thyroid, glandular
Heart	Heart failure, asthma
Solar Plexus	Arthritis, gastric and dietary disorders, diabetes, indigestion,
Sacral	Ob/gyn problems, urinary
Base or Root	Depression, immune and sexual disorders

chakra. Some years ago I suffered from a throat chakra imbalance and even today this remains an area of my energy that I have to be aware of. Being eager to please and make others happy, I did not find it easy to express feelings of anger or dissatisfaction. In point of fact, I knew that there was no need for me to be feeling that way, that I was suffering from an ego-related issue of perception that I allowed myself to become angry over. However, in spite of being aware of the issue, I allowed the anger to occur. As a result, my energy clogged up in my throat and I

CHAKRA	ASSOCIATED EMOTION
Crown	Values, ethics, selflessness, inspiration, spirituality, devotion
Third Eye	Truth, intellectual abilities, learning from experience, emotional intelligence, wisdom, vision
Throat	Will, addiction, judgement, faith, decision-making
Heart	Love, grief, anger, forgiveness, compassion, hope
Solar Plexus	Trust, self-confidence, responsibility
Sacral	Creativity, guilt, blame, control, ethics, honour
Base or Root	Tribal, safety, instincts, family

regularly suffered from loss of voice or what appeared to be 'throat infections'. Once I received some healing which helped to unravel all of the issues behind my so-called sore throats, I became aware of the problem and found ways to tackle it through my way of perceiving. Treating my throat with crystals, hands-on healing and essential oils meant that I shifted the condition once and for all, and have never suffered from it since.

There is also a perfectly natural shift of energetic focus upwards through the energy body and the chakras during life. The focus upon each chakra tends to shift quite uniformly every seven years, give or take a little, so that the energies and the physical and emotional issues related to them will tend to bring each inidividual's focus to bear on certain physical or emotional issues. This happens as a result of the process of emotional and mental

The focus upon each chakra can shift quite uniformly every seven years, give or take a little.

development that takes place through our energy field. Because of the chakras' presence at an emotional body level, the energetic frequencies involved with each chakra have certain emotional issues related to them. So an influx of energy, for example, in your root chakra at an emotional body level will tend to bring issues of instinct and the need to provide to the fore. At a physical level, this could manifest as any one of a number of symptoms such as lower back pain and to a certain degree, problems with sexual organs.

The energetic shift upwards can also occur far more quickly than every seven years depending upon one's own development, or much more slowly. Often, my clients are people who have got 'stuck' in one chakra and are just not moving forward in their own development and life. There are even personality 'types' who get stuck in their energetic development; the kind of men who seem to have the same emotional development as little boys are often stuck in their second chakras and oscillate between the second and throat chakras as their energy naturally fights to find a way to move upwards. This personality type is one that tends to be very creative but lacks the willpower to bring projects to fruition. These people also like to feel powerful and protective around others, but actually feel they need protection (usually under their mother's apron!). They can also be very bullish about controlling their independence and having their own way, yet demand that everyone else drops everything to fit in with them when they suddenly need help. The physical problems related to these emotional conditions tend to manifest as lower-back pain and muscular weakness in that area, an over- or underactive sex drive (usually a swing between the two), bladder problems, mouth ulcers, and throat or neck pain.

There are a great many ways to help to keep your energy system clear, fully functioning and vital.

THE HUMAN EXPERIENCE

You can work with your chakras in a huge variety of ways to bring about release and shift of your own energies and find ways in which to heal. Many of the ways in which we can work with chakra energies are related to our physical senses. Because each chakra is a band of energetic frequencies, they can be perceived or understood in any way that the human brain is capable of processing energetic vibrations and input via the sensory organs. This is the key to understanding how vibrational (or energy) medicine can help to move your energy. Each band of frequencies related to a given chakra can be perceived as the colour of light with which it resonates; as well as sounds, scents, and even thoughts.

There are a great many ways to help to keep your energy system clear, fully functioning and vital, and we will look later in the book at ways to use widely available energy medicines such as essential oils, crystals, and flower remedies. However, there is a beautiful and straightforward form of energy medicine that is available to almost all of us, and one that we can use as a powerful way of raising awareness

Most of us think in words, so one of the simplest and most powerful forms of medicine known to man is sound.

of our own issues on a physical, emotional, and mental level: language.

It's important to recognise just how powerful language can be as a tool for change and for raising self-awareness. The term 'language' embraces myriad forms of communication and so means many things to many people, whether it is spoken, written, or even body language. But for the sake of this book, the easiest and most comprehensive way to use language as a diagnostic and healing tool is simply to think about our own spoken and written communication. Most of us think in words, so one of the simplest and most powerful forms of medicine known to man is sound. Sound is something that almost all of us can access by using our own voices and ability to hear. And far from excluding those who are unable to vocalise or those who have hearing difficulties, let me reassure you that sound works, as all holistic medicine does, on a vibrational level. After all, sound is just a frequency of energetic vibration that we can perceive with certain senses but of course, sound exists regardless of whether you can hear it sitting next to me, and I have my fingers in my ears so I can't. Though of course, in healing work it helps to focus your awareness on the tools that you are using to shift your energy; the vibration will have an effect regardless of whether you choose to be aware of the presence of the sound or not.

THE ENERGY OF LANGUAGE

There are a number of theories about where language comes from and how human beings first began to make noises or commonly used sounds as labels for objects and ideas. Any use of spoken or written language involves having a brain that can 'conceptualise'; that can understand thinking in symbols – which is what the letters that make up our language are. So the basis of language is to apply a picture or mark of some kind to an object or idea; to some kind of event.

Our energy system is constantly interacting at a very deep level with the world around us. Just as it is here that we experience disturbances before they are manifested on a physical level, we perceive the world

with our energy before we ever register a sensation physically with our senses. All of us have walked into a room, or met another person, or visited a place, and at a very deep level, before making a visual judgement, registered that this place, person or situation 'feels good' or 'doesn't feel right'. When that happens, your brain is making sense of a registering of sensation within

Occasionally, you will also find that other people's chakra energies hook into your own.

your energy field. Humans tend to use the energy of the solar plexus chakra to sense out people and situations quite naturally; it's a little like having an energetic early warning system. Hence the term, 'gut feeling'!

Strictly speaking, the feelings you register as a result of sensing with your solar plexus energy are likely to be emotionally based and in the medium term, they may turn out not to be correct or fair; but this is how the human energy system works. It gives our physical bodies the necessary caution to just stand back a little until we can make a more valid decision about what it is we ought to do for our own safety. Occasionally, you will also find that other people's chakra energies hook into your own. This can be in a very pleasant way, for example if you meet someone you feel really 'in tune' with. It can also be quite an unpleasant experience, as when one meets people who feel as though

The heart chakra, for example, tends to correspond with energies that are related to our sense of touch and emotions of love.

they are pulling us in, or drawing from us – I call people who habitually do this to others 'sappers'. These people literally drain you, and you can part company with them feeling quite exhausted.

So whenever you perceive an aspect of your world, you first feel it way 'out there', at the level of your abstract mental energy on an energetic level. The physical senses that human beings have and make use of to understand our energetic sensations are what enable our brains to process information and act upon it accordingly. The human brain itself is constantly evolving, and a very early part of it is known as the limbic brain, sometimes called the 'lizard brain', due to its ancient nature. This part of the brain is concerned with the perception and processing of sensory information as it is received, and is the place where the brain decides what to 'do' with it in processing terms. Some senses are more closely associated with some chakras than with others because the energetic frequencies within those chakras resonate more freely with the energies within certain of our sensory processing mechanisms. The heart chakra, for example, tends to correspond with energies that are related to our sense of touch and emotions of love.

On a more general level, the information that we perceive via our energy field through the senses is subject to a sorting process within the limbic brain. This determines whether the information we're receiving is relevant to a feeling, a smell, a colour, or a sound; so the limbic brain is almost working directly off pure energy. This is one of the ways in which energy can be understood as having an information-carrying capacity, or simply 'being' information. A condition even exists known as 'synesthesia' in which people process information quite differently and will, for example, smell colours or taste words. This is currently thought to occur due to a mismatching of information from sense organs through the functioning of the limbic brain which is also thought to be the part of the brain where we initially relate a 'feeling' or perception to its label, or word sound as we will later process it within the 'higher' functons of the brain. So, the sensation we perceive becomes something we can explain with language.

Within the human energy field the labelling, or the concept of relating words to given perceptions, takes place at the level of the concrete mental energy. Within the abstract mental body there are thoughts, perceptions, and sensations that do not have a label or concept associated with them. Learn the concept that a rectangular object with four legs has the name 'table', however, and the concept becomes a concrete understanding. This will be used in future experiences to understand that other, similar objects are also called tables. Through the

Events that occur in the outside world will be registered within a particular chakra.

process of perceiving, processing, and relating a label or symbol to a concept, ideas can become fixed within the concrete mental body and thus have an effect on the emotional and physical energy. In other words, I can learn that I can place objects safely upon a table; so I will persist in placing objects quite naturally and happily upon tables. This process is a great learning tool but can also be used to our detriment. For example, I can learn that the concept of my face and body are labelled with the words 'fat' and 'ugly'. This concept can become so fixed that, even when slim and looking wonderful, my inner conceptual pattern will still relate those labels to my physical appearance. The emotional effects of this kind of detrimental energy pattern are clear. The physical effects could be anything from excessive dieting to an eating disorder.

Because each chakra resonates with certain energetic vibrations, the events that occur in the outside world will also be registered within a particular chakra or chakras. For example, the 'gut feeling' of fear relates to a set of vibrations felt within the root (instinct) and solar plexus (emotion) chakras. The way in which those frequencies are processed and understood within the brain, will be registered as an intellectual–emotional response like panic, anger, and so on. That sense of fear might even cause us to utter a physical sound related to the emotional sensation, like a scream, or make a physical action, like running away. Some people might 'see red'. So you can begin to see how the energetic vibrations relating to each

Early language consisted of nothing more complex than a set of shared sounds.

chakra can be processed as, for example, a sound, a colour, or a scent, depending upon the propensity for information processing predominant in that individual, or most appropriate to the way that the information is received.

THE POWER OF THE SPOKEN WORD

So, each chakra relates, not only to a verbal/auditory vibration (a sound), but also to a note. We'll consider sound as a healing therapy in the next chapter, but for now, just remember that the simple concept of sounds relating to each chakra's energy is the key to understanding language.

CHAKRA	ASSOCIATED SOUND
Crown	EEE
Third Eye	AYE
Throat	EYE
Heart	AH
Solar Plexus	OH
Sacral	OOO
Base or Root	UH

For example, an event in the outside world relating to the root chakra energies would cause me to register a sensation and I, in attempting to express or communicate that event with others, would make the sound appropriately produced by the brain and relayed to the verbal organs. If a lion attacked me, I would scream. So, the concept of labelling an event would occur – a scream sound matching a fearful, root chakra event. Likewise, another human being might begin to understand the same concept because they register common sensations and emotional responses – as you do when you 'know how someone is feeling'.

Listen to or record yourself speaking and see where you place your own emphasis in terms of energy and language.

Early language consisted of nothing more complex than a set of shared sounds, with no shape being given to that sound in terms of a language or word label. Later, the need to differentiate between sounds, and the need to explain, for example, the difference between a lion attacking

and a spider landing on me, would necessitate the use of labels. Clearly, the vowel sounds that stimulate the chakras vary slightly from one culture and language to another but are often in essence remarkably similar, as are the vowel sounds used in healing work throughout very different cultures the world over.

All of this goes to show where the

words each of us tends to favour come from, how we come to like or dislike using certain words, and how many of us get our names. Babies turn up with a predominance of one kind of energy, for example an excess of crown chakra energy – and will be named for it, purely on the basis of how people sensing the presence of that baby respond to their energy. In the case of the

throat chakra energy, I used the note 'G' and words that sounded like 'eye'. One of the most powerful healing phrases is 'I am' and of course 'I' is a way of verbalising your own strength and identity, an exercise which is particularly related to issues of not communicating or expressing one's own feelings. So for me, reaffirming 'my' and 'I' sentences helped to move and resonate with the energy that had been stuck in that chakra. I also worked less intensively with word sounds up and down the other chakras to help to balance the energy that I was moving. Try it yourself by looking at whether you use a predominance of words relating to one or more particular chakras. Then refer to the charts on physical and emotional issues (see pp. 62–4) to

crown chakra, this is likely to be a name with an 'eee' sound in it. Sometimes, we get the naming process wrong, or the people around a baby have 'decided' a name before that child is born, which is why some people don't like or 'feel like' their names, or want to change the names they were originally given, later on in life.

Becoming aware of the kind of language you habitually use, and the emotions and chakra energies related to it, can be an interesting and illuminating exercise. Listen to or record yourself speaking and see where you habitually place your own emphasis in terms of energy and language. This will also help you to understand where you tend to put unresolved emotions within your physical body. To move my own

Remember at all times that self-healing is not about struggle, hassle, pain, guilt, or recriminations.

see whether you are experiencing any of those issues associated with the chakras your language is most active in. You can then try to balance it by working with sounds from other chakras.

HEALING THROUGH LANGUAGE

This process gives you infinite choice to bring about your own powerful healing and make conscious choices about the ways in which you can change. For example, if you are someone who tends to focus your energies in your lower chakras, and would like to bring some of your energies into your heart and higher chakras, you could begin to change your language to include the higher chakra sounds and words – for example by using 'eee' sounds in preference to 'uh' and 'oh'. Some people even sing songs or chant mantras to help shift their energies to other chakras. You can choose the ways in which you would like to bring new energies into your life, and the benefits you would like to enjoy, or ways in which you want to alter your current situation, and start to shift them very simply for yourself.

I cannot emphasise enough how powerful this approach can be and the speed, simplicity and clarity with which you can influence emotional and physical change within your life. Please do remember at all times though, that self-healing is not about struggle, hassle, pain, guilt, or recriminations. In other words, don't start beating yourself up if you find yourself slipping back, forgetting to make changes in your language, and so on. All of that will add to your frustration. Remember – you're not trying to improve yourself or to reach an unattainable perfect spiritual state. You are already there! All you're doing is peeling away the layers of your onion, letting go of useless patterns of energy, and allowing yourself to be an expression of the soul energy that you already are.

Language clearly provides a powerful and easily accessible tool for raising your own awareness, for energetic diagnoses.

Language clearly provides a powerful and easily accessible tool for raising your own awareness, for energetic diagnoses. Awareness of and changing your use of language can help bring about a profound shift on an emotional level in terms of the way you feel about and express, or

CASE STUDY

WORKING WITH LANGUAGE

I worked with a client some years ago who suffered from panic attacks due to a root chakra problem. Part of her healing process involved working with simple, soft, 'aaaah' sounds of the heart chakra to help move her energy to a calmer level and release the energy from the root chakra energy and her sensation of irrational fear. She worked with the word 'heart' with a long 'aaaaah' sound in it – 'heaaaaaaart'; and a series of other words that she used to make up sentences whenever she found herself experiencing sensations of panic. For instance, she would say, 'Aaaah, deaaaar, sweetheaaaart', and even recite rhymes like 'baaa, baaa, black sheep'. These word sounds served to focus her energy up to her heart and crown chakras, relieving the sensation of balled-up panic in her root chakra. Christine found that, after a while, she no longer needed to sit and focus on the words she was using to bring her energy up to her heart chakra, she could simply think the sounds silently to herself. She adopted the habit of using more 'aah' sounds in her language and it was remarkable to witness the speed with which her panic attacks were released as her energies moved from her root chakra.

conversely, feel about the way you express your world to others and thus, your mental, emotional and physical health. Appreciating the value of this process is what much of the practice of NLP (neuro-linguistic programming) is based upon. Remembering the premise of the interconnectedness of all life, what you see is what you choose to see, and what you express, you attract. Put more simply, 'as you think, so shall you be'. Intent to act, as always, is the basic expression of your physical being, because intent expresses physical existence and action. So, by understanding the way in which you currently perceive,

understand, relate to, and then express your view of the world, you can increase your understanding of yourself, your issues, and how to heal and release them by attracting a different energetic pattern into your life. By changing your thoughts and the words with which you think them, you can reinforce new patterns of being as a means of bringing about your own healing.

Next, we look at how musical sound can be used to help release and heal energetic patterns within the chakra system, along with other simple vibrational medicines such as crystals, essential oils, colour, and homeopathic flower remedies.

ANALYSE YOUR LANGUAGE

Make a list of words or phrases you favour (you might listen to yourself talking to others, record yourself in conversation, write down a passage as it comes into your head, or look at letters or e-mails you have written).

Relate these words, through their vowel sounds, to the chakras (see chart, p.62-3).

Do you concentrate certain words around the energy of specific chakras?

Do you change your language and word use according to your mood? This might tell you where you tend to focus your energies when you are in different moods.

USING LANGUAGE TO EFFECT CHANGE

Stop focusing on the favourite words you are currently working with and choose some relating to other chakras to balance your energies.

To rebalance your energies you can choose words appropriate to any other chakra and make them a part of your everyday vocabulary. Or, you can choose one word for each chakra and make an exercise of sitting and repeating each word for a couple of minutes two or three times a day.

USING SOUND TO HEAL PROBLEMS

For an imbalance of the physical/emotional related to one particular chakra, you can focus on working with the note/vowel sound for that chakra.

Let's now look at practical and simp[...]
can use the energy of some tools and [...]
under the heading of 'vibrational medicin[...]
release and thus heal from within your ene[...]
Each of these therapies provides ways in whi[...]
with your chakras and energy field from a physi[...]
emotional, and mental level through to your soul level
energy. In this book, my aim is to offer simple ways of
working to release and heal energy on the deepest levels.
So, where you feel you need more in-depth information or

CHAPTER 4

Awakening

are interested to find out more about a given therapy, do
refer to specialist books on each topic. What I have
attempted to do here is to present a basic approach to
working with each of the energetic tools that I'm going to
summarise, in terms of my own experience of their
usefulness and accessibility to all of us. You can go out and
buy the necessary tools in most high streets, without need
for specialist suppliers. With each approach I've also
included a list of the chakras that the individual elements
of each therapy are appropriate to, along with, where
possible, a note of the energetic issues that each therapy
can help to release. You might find these useful in helping
you to choose the appropriate key to the pattern you
would like to release.

Energy medicines such as sound, work primarily on the energy field and chakras and can thus affect the physical body. Some vibrational tools, such as essential oils, also have a direct physical effect, but they work through the physical body via the senses. Each can help to move energetic patterns that are no longer

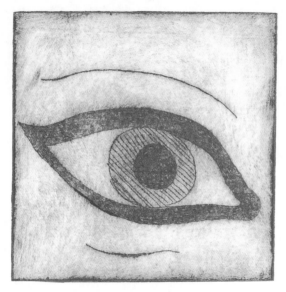

useful to you and help you to reach a level of greater peace and clarity.

In the last chapter, I talked a little about the role of the senses with which we perceive our world and the information-processing capacity of the limbic or 'lizard' brain. Our senses are the physical means with which we perceive the energetic input from the physical world around us in terms of vibrational energy – light and colour, sounds, scent, taste,

and so on. Energy medicines work directly though the energy body but can also be perceived with the senses of the physical body, so they offer a wonderfully rounded or holistic approach to your health as a multi-dimensional energetic being.

The senses provide a key or a way in for healing vibrational medicines to reach deeper levels of our human experience, thereby helping to release a little more of that held energy that might have been keeping us stuck. It's also fun and in many ways delightful to work with sensually pleasing tools as a way to raise our own energetic vibration and awareness.

THE TOOLS OF INTENT

Always remember that any energy medicine that you work with is a tool to harness and amplify your healing intent. That's not to say that the remedies will not work unless you 'programme' them, which is a common misapprehension behind energy medicine using crystals. Each of us takes responsibility for our own healing; so unless we are ready to heal, the healing will not take place. Vibrational medicines offer a way of peeling the onion, to find a way in to the energies that underlie what we perceive as our 'presenting' problems. So, it is important to be aware that your intent when working with energetic medicines can greatly add to the power of the medicines themselves. If you also work with hands-on healing of any kind, always give the tools you are working with – oils, crystals, or homeopathic remedy – a good blast of healing energy before using them, as this will help to increase their efficacy.

Vibrational medicines aim to begin to move your energy from a physical level, through your emotional energy body to bring spiritual or soul level energies into your normal awareness. Where your energy is blocked at, for example, a physical level, this is not only a manifestation of an energetic issue but also a continuing block to that energy working to help you in a beneficial way. All healing is simply letting go. This might mean that you experience a number of related symptoms connected with your release process through using vibrational medicines. Increased or suddenly vivid sequences of dreams, for example, are a form of release from the unconscious mind. Dreams will be discussed in a later chapter so please refer to that for more information, but for the time being, remain aware of your experiences and make notes whenever you have an interesting dream. Other symptoms that you may experience include remembering events that you thought you had forgotten, along with any related emotions. Do bear the process of release in mind as you

work with your chosen remedies, because nothing is stranger than experiencing sudden mental confusion, or a sequence of mood swings for no apparent reason. All energy medicines can also trigger a recurrence of old physical conditions as they are 'kicked out' or released. If you are ever in any doubt, always consult your doctor or other medical adviser.

RELEASING AND HEALING

When it comes to dealing with the mental and emotional release that can take place, it may be useful to have someone to talk it over with on an unconditional basis. Talk to your

Do bear the process of release in mind as you work with your chosen remedies.

friends or family or, if it is more appropriate, go to a counsellor who can help you to deal with what it is you're experiencing. If you prefer, you can keep a journal of your healing process and write down what you experience. This can be invaluable as a reference at a later date as you begin to make deeper sense of what you're releasing, and it can help you to understand the way in which your healing pattern relates to energy that has been held within different layers of your energy field.

Always remember that any form of release is just another layer of your own consciousness being worked through, in order to heal the deeper energy underlying the problem you are currently aware of. If you're starting with a physical issue, you may well begin to work through underlying emotional levels of energy that you have been holding. Don't worry – it is a positive process. I always liken clearing and releasing processes to doing the washing – it might not be the most fun in the world at the time, but it feels wonderful afterwards! Handle any clearance in a positive manner and you'll find the whole process far less

Don't worry – it is a positive process. I always liken clearing and releasing processes to doing the washing.

painful than if you approach it with trepidation. It's all part of the journey of exploration; you're plumbing the depths of your being on the way to your soul, to learn to let go of the patterns and cycles that you have been holding on to and are currently experiencing. It's also worth mentioning that not everyone experiences the clearance process on a conscious level, or is particularly aware of the process of releasing, so don't panic if you find the whole process to be plain sailing. In the end

whatever is right for you will happen and with most vibrational medicines there is nothing dangerous or harmful that you can do so long as you follow the guidelines given. If you are in any doubt, ask an expert.

DOWSING FOR YOUR REMEDY
With each of the forms of therapy given here, I have included some 'diagnostics', or ways that you can determine which is the appropriate remedy to use, or which you would prefer to use. However, this can actually engage you in a process of decision about which remedy to use on an intellectual level, that might involve your judgement of yourself and your symptoms. So, there are also a couple of easy intuitive techniques that you can learn and apply in order to select a remedy on a judgement-free basis! The first is dowsing. Anyone can dowse; it is just a case of using a tool (your pendulum) to amplify something that, at a deeper level, you already know. People often watch others dowsing and say, 'but I can see you moving the pendulum!'. Of course the hand holding the pendulum will move it; often almost imperceptibly, sometimes quite dramatically. The pendulum is not being pushed by an outside force, it's being used as a means of arriving at an answer to your question, through the tiny signals that are given by the

subconscious mind to the physical body. This is not to say that you should ever influence a pendulum consciously; but just let your body do with it what it wants to do and if you notice your hand moving, let it go!

To begin dowsing, first, find yourself a pendulum. You can make one just by tying a piece of string around a stone or any other small weight that will swing. Then, holding your pendulum over a neutral surface like the floor or a table (i.e. not your own body – you can pick up vibrations of energy from your knees, for example), ask your pendulum to 'show me yes'. Don't attempt to 'fix' your hand but at the same time, don't purposely move it in any given direction. Your pendulum will move either in a clockwise or anti-clockwise circle, move back and forth away from you, or move horizontally in front of you. It should feel almost as though it is being 'swung' for you. Then, ask your pendulum to 'show me no'. It will generally make the opposite movement. My pendulums always swing in a clockwise circle for yes, and anti-clockwise for no. You can also ask for a neutral answer, though in point of fact, a neutral answer will generally be no movement at all or very little obvious movement. Don't worry about the size of your pendulum's swing, either – this does not in any way denote a more or less positive response. So,

when you come to choosing your remedy, hold your pendulum above the crystal, oil, flower remedy, piece of coloured card or cloth, or whatever it is you want an answer about. Then, ask a yes or no question – 'Is this the remedy I need?' Incidentally, you can dowse for

anything – to find out where you have lost something, to ask questions about events in your life, what to eat for dinner, what clothes to wear, which TV programme to watch, and so on.

ENERGY-TESTING REMEDIES
Another technique for selecting a remedy is known as 'muscle-testing', or 'energy-testing'. It comes from a field of energy therapy called kinesiology which is both a

therapeutic and diagnostic tool in itself, and which can be studied over a period of time to gain a recognised qualification. Energy-testing can be used to check whether the remedy in which you are interested is appropriate, but you do need someone else to help test you. What you are testing with this technique is whether the remedy you select is one that your body will resist, or work with. I have been energy-tested by an homeopath to select a remedy in this way.

The subject of the test (i.e. yourself, if you are selecting remedies for your own use) should stand with the left arm held out sideways from the body, horizontal to the ground. First, there is a neutral test in which the subject resists the pressure of the tester's hand, while the tester pushes down gently but firmly on the subject's hand, just for a moment, having asked a neutral question like, 'Is your name …?' This will show you the kind of resistance you have naturally within your energy field, without a remedy affecting your system.

Then, the remedy or a series of remedies is tested. Hold the remedy you are going to test in your closed hand and again, the tester will momentarily press down on your hand, asking 'Is this the remedy you need?' It can be more helpful if you are unaware of which remedy is in

your hand, so as to ensure that the results are based on energy alone and not on anything you may know or decide intellectually. The remedy your body needs will be the one that is most in tune with your system and should show a greater degree of 'dip' in your arm when pressed – in other words, less resistance. The variations in resistance from one remedy to another may be only slight or they may be quite dramatic.

The remedy your body needs will be the one that is most in tune with your system.

You can also use energy-testing to check for foods you might be allergic to; ask the question, 'Am I allergic to this substance?' – the one that most affects your body will produce a greater dip than the neutral test. Or, you can test for areas of the body that have an imbalance of energy, for example the site of an old injury; ask the question, 'Does this area need healing?'

So, in terms of remedies that are easily available, let's remember that each chakra or energy centre vibrates at certain frequencies, and will resonate with certain specific remedies on the same frequencies as itself. Some vibrational therapies even fall broadly into a natural division of seven parts that correspond to each of the seven main chakras. This, for example includes notes within the octave of music and colours of light within the spectrum, so these therapies are the simplest to begin to understand and work with. Other tools like crystals incorporate both light and colour energy as well as a very fast energetic vibrational frequency of their own that some people claim to be able to 'hear'. Essential oils, which have both colour and scent, along with the energy of plants in the form of flower remedies, also include the original colour of the living flower.

Following on from our investigation into the use of language in the last chapter, let's start our tour of energy medicines with a look at the therapeutic use of sound.

HEALING WITH SOUND

Having examined the role of the limbic brain in processing the information received through energy in the last chapter, let's now take a moment to remember that energy has an information-carrying capacity. The energy that we perceive can be processed in a number of ways via our sense organs and brain. As nothing more complex than

... ask yourself the question, 'Does this area need healing?'

vibrations, or frequencies of energy, sound can have a deep and profound effect on the human psyche. It is said that the basic, creative sound energy of the universe can be heard as a hum, often called 'aum' or 'ohm'. Methods of healing through sound are still used in Buddhist, American Indian, Hindu and Aboriginal cultures and among pygmy tribes of the rainforests, as well as by professional therapists in the Western world. Many of the ancient spiritual chants, mantras and songs of these cultures come from healing sounds that are found to stimulate the energy of the body to healing itself. Shamans drum, monks chant and witchdoctors whoop, all in the name of healing. Think of the effects that, for example, chalk being squeaked down an old-fashioned blackboard can have on the way you feel, or, the way in which the sound of a crying baby can alert or disturb you. Noticing the effects of sounds that you experience in daily life will help to raise your awareness of sound's potential as a therapy or medicine.

Several sound-healing systems (including primordial sound

CHAKRA	ASSOCIATED MANTRA
Crown	Aum
Third Eye	Om
Throat	Ham
Heart	Yam
Solar Plexus	Ram
Sacral	Vam
Base or Root	Lam

techniques as used in Ayurvedic healing; Indian mantra yoga; the Healing Voice School), work on the chakras and leading modern experts have identified notes that can be used to help rebalance the chakra energy. You are probably well aware of the revitalising properties of lively music, and how a cheerful song can really lift your mood. Conversely you might find yourself depressed by monotonous or dull-sounding music, or music that is played at an offensively loud volume. Studies have even been carried out on the effect that music has on the growth of plants, showing that seeds respond

most favourably to gentle, harmonious refrains, but actually grow away from and have their growth stunted by harsh and loud music. So, if the growth and basic health of an organism as simple as a plant are affected in this way, just imagine the powerful effects that music and sound can have upon us as human beings!

Sound is not only a means of expressing energy, but also of manipulating and moving it. Try experimenting with different kinds of 'mood' music to discover which has a calming effect, which energises you, which makes you laugh and want to move to the rhythm, and which depresses or saddens you. Research into the effects of sound stimulating the auditory nerve and how it resonates within the brain shows that used correctly, sound can heal, but used in an aggressive way, it can actually harm. None of the suggestions in this book, however, will cause you any damage.

One way to start to release energy blockages for yourself through sound is to buy some healing music and listen to it or even just have it playing in the background. There are some wonderful recordings now available of 'inner healing' chants sung by Tibetan Buddhist monks. They sing with what is known as the 'one voice chord'. It is said that only monks who have attained enlightenment are physically able to sing the one voice chord – they literally sing several notes at a time to produce a harmonic chord with a bass, treble and top note; a sound that has to be experienced to be believed. This is one form of music

that really does have an immediate and powerful effect upon the mind and body. It is thought that healing chants like these can actually recharge your energy from a blocked, depleted or underactive state, or from a state of excessive activity, to a balanced, flowing and harmonious condition in which you feel 'in tune' with yourself.

CHAKRA BALANCING WITH SOUND

Another way to balance your own energy through the use of sound is by singing the notes that correspond to the chakras you would like to

balance. You can do this in the car, in bed, cooking a meal, or walking the dogs. If you don't know which notes correspond to the letters on the diagram below, you can try using a tuning fork that will be labelled with the correct letter and, when struck, will produce the sound for you. If you know someone who has a musical instrument or can sing, they could record the sounds for you. It's easy enough to make your own energy-balancing tape of chakra sounds or a tape from which you can learn to sound the notes.

'Sounding' is a therapeutic singing technique that involves focusing on one chakra at a time.

'Sounding' is a therapeutic singing technique that involves focusing on one chakra at a time, and producing the note that will balance it for a whole, deep breath, before pausing and moving on to the next chakra.

CHAKRA	ASSOCIATED NOTE
Crown	B flat
Third Eye	A
Throat	G
Heart	F sharp
Solar Plexus	E
Sacral	D
Base or Root	C

Generally speaking, allowing yourself time to experience harmonious and relaxing music on a regular basis can be beneficial to your mental and emotional wellbeing. Recordings made specifically for relaxation and meditation are wonderfully calming to have playing in the background as you enjoy relaxing pastimes such as reading or gardening, or a creative activity such as painting or cooking, or even as you lie still and let your mind wander. Even twenty minutes spent lying still listening to some relaxing music can slow your heart rate and brain activity to the point where your body is allowed to recharge its batteries. A point of interest to note is that I have seen sound therapy have some deep healing effects even upon those who cannot hear it.

HEALING WITH COLOUR

The music and light concerts that have been put on as a feast for the senses throughout the centuries, right up to modern times are healing in themselves. Light, as sound, is a frequency of energy and so can have

CASE STUDY

USING SOUND TO HEAL THE DEAF

I was recently called in to treat a child who is profoundly deaf and incapable of hearing any sound at all. Cally was deeply depressed and withdrawn to the point of appearing autistic to the people with whom she came into contact, but in fact she was a deeply sensitive, bright and active child when she felt happy, who was full of love and a bubbling sense of joy. It occurred to me that Cally's withdrawal was somehow related to her silent world and I remembered an occasion when my husband had blown a conch shell that had an enlivening effect on a friend's deaf dog. The dog had simply felt the sound vibrations and become wildly excited; so I tried the same principle with Cally. Sure enough, a look of utter delight lit up her face as I blew into the shell and she instantly leapt up and down trying to touch the shell and look into it to see where the sensations she was feeling came from. For the first time in several months, Cally laughed and she even started to dance. We experimented with sound and found that the ones that cheered her up, and that she enjoyed most, were the conch shell, a Tibetan clearing bell, a natural drum made from a hollowed-out tree stump, and a pair of cymbals. She takes great delight in dancing with her cymbals herself now and the sudden shift and healing in her condition as a result of such a simple therapy has not only been lasting, but has brought out a side of Cally that was previously only glimpsed at fleetingly.

PRACTISE SOUNDING

This straightforward sound rebalancing exercise can be done at any time of day, but if you're using it as a healing method, you should try and work through it once or, if possible, twice a day for seven days. Thereafter, use it whenever you need or want to. If you are working to release physical, emotional or mental symptoms related to a particular chakra, simply use the note related to that chakra to help to move your energy – and get ready for the clearance process! This technique is particularly calming and energising if someone else does it for you or if you can do it for someone else, standing in front of them and sounding each note up through the seven main chakras until you reach the crown.

Take several deep, relaxed breaths before you begin, so that your chest and upper body are relaxed, and your head is held with your chin away from your chest but in a relaxed and flexible way. It helps if you stand to sing.

Slowly and with your eyes closed, take a single breath and begin to sing a root chakra 'C'. Hold the sound for as long as you can without breaking it, breathing out into the note. Feel how the sound changes as you produce it and also any effects within your body and mind on your mood, emotions, or the thoughts that come into your head.

When you finish your breath, let the note go, and pause to take a couple of deep, relaxed breaths before moving up to a sacral chakra note.

If you can, after singing a crown chakra note, use one breath to let your voice fall gently down through all the notes again as a grounding exercise.

Experiment with the recommended notes for each chakra, but be aware that you may find other notes that you find more comfortable to use for particular chakras.

a therapeutic effect on the body just by being present. As with sound, the healing benefits will be there even if you don't look at the colours we see as light, but they are greatly enhanced if you do! Colour, of course, does not actually exist as a concrete element of the outside world. The colour that we perceive is the way that our brains process the light that we see; you see a colour that is the frequency of light reflected by the object you are looking at (it absorbs every other colour of light).

The frequencies of energy that resonate within each chakra can also be perceived as colour. So, it's a simple enough matter to match a colour with a chakra and so balance the energies you are seeing to move and heal. It is often said that certain colours have an 'enlivening' or 'depressing' effect, but this will depend entirely on the subject experiencing exposure to the colour and their own energetic condition at a given time. Effects also vary with the tone of the colour; for example, a bright, acid yellow tends to have a stimulating effect upon our mental activity and lift our mood. A creamier yellow can often be thought of as 'mellow' and can have a calming, gentle effect that is still happy enough for a therapy room. A muddy, ochre yellow can have quite a dulling, depressing effect.

Healers have been using colour therapy since time immemorial to lift the energies and bring about a

> *The frequencies of energy that resonate within each chakra can also be perceived as colour. So, it's a simple enough matter to match a colour with a chakra.*

shift in the healing processes. Professional colour therapists work with instruments that shine light through coloured filters, and other equipment to expose the body to the desired colour resonance for therapeutic purposes. However, all of our lives are filled with colour, from the clothes we wear, to the décor in our homes, the plants in our garden, our choice of office equipment, and even the food we eat. A most powerful way to help release

CHAKRA	ASSOCIATED COLOUR
Crown	Violet, white
Third Eye	Indigo
Throat	Blue
Heart	Green, rose
Solar Plexus	Yellow
Sacral	Orange
Base or Root	Red

and enhance your own energies is to focus upon the colour with which you surround yourself on a daily basis.

COLOUR THERAPY FOR THE HOME

Ideally you should have spaces within your home painted a variety of different colours so that whenever you feel the need to boost flagging energies, you can spend some time around the colour you need to lift your mood. This is not always entirely practical or possible, or even aesthetically desirable, but it is as well to be aware that the colours with which you surround yourself can have a profound effect upon your mood and thus, your health. When I bought my last house, the living room was painted such a deep Suffolk-pink colour as to be almost red. I found the colour quite draining and depressing, primarily because it's really a root chakra colour and my energies tend to be much more top-end, faster and higher. It was fine for grounding for short periods of time, but could leave you feeling sleepy, angry, and miserable if you spent long periods of time in that room.

I ended up with areas of all the chakra colours and particularly the ones that I found most enhanced my own energy in that little house: the outside was painted a lilac colour (third eye and crown chakra energy and about spiritual development), with a bright turquoise door (meta-heart or truth chakra, to do with speaking your truths, and finding your true spiritual way in this world). This was most appropriate, although at the time we opted for the turquoise door, we didn't know why it was that we were attracted to it. Inside, the dining room was painted a deep emerald green (heart chakra) along with a bright lime green (also heart chakra but a lighter vibration, and white (crown/whole energy system). Our living room was lilac and silver (third eye and crown); the

Spend some time around the colour you need to lift your mood.

kitchen was pink (heart) and pale blue (throat); the study area, where I worked and wrote much of the time, was bright yellow to stimulate mental activity, along with red to ground the information I was working with, and orange (sacral chakra, for creative energy). Our bedroom was pale blue and white, very heavenly and top-end for communication and all-over soothing, peaceful energy. So right through the house, we had colours we could access to balance ourselves whenever we felt we needed to.

For a short period between homes we stayed in a house decorated with dusky shades of orange and peach and beige – nothing bright anywhere. Finding it quite a downer visually and in terms of my energy, the first thing I did on moving in was to bring in lots of bright plants and have little spots of colour wherever I could. Now my home is almost totally white, which reflects a lighter and more peaceful atmosphere. If you find yourself struggling or feeling odd in a

particular room of your house, ask someone to energy-test you – 'Is this a colour I need?' – or to dowse in each room, or even over pots of paint, pieces of coloured card or cloth. It need not be difficult or expensive to alter your environment – you might try something as simple as a brightly coloured plant pot or flowering plant, or a bright set of

pens or pencils, a paperweight on your desk, a picture on the wall, a bottle of bubble-bath, or a vase of flowers. If you find that you have issues related to certain chakras, focus on using the appropriate colours to help to shift and release the energy within them.

THE CHALLENGE OF CHAKRA-DRESSING

Most of us choose the colours we wear according to those we feel we need to get us through the day, but occasionally we wear colours that relate to the energetic blockages we experience most often. If you habitually dress in or buy certain colours, dowse or energy test to determine whether you're wearing a colour you need, or a colour that is working against you. It has to be said that this is really not for devout fashion victims. People who are particularly in touch with their energy will go out wearing the most outrageous displays of colour, without a concern for how they look, just because they feel those colours are what they want to be around that day. Hence the syndrome of the man who goes out with a yellow shirt, turquoise trousers and pink socks; it might be a visual shock for those with their energies in other places, but it could be just what the guy who is wearing that outfit needs! This is also something that children do, and in general we all try to avoid something we feel really terrible wearing. I like to wear the odd touch of something like silver which I find lifts me and brings my energies up. If you're experiencing problems with the energy related to a particular chakra, wear clothes in the colours of the energy you need to move.

FOOD THERAPY

We've all heard chefs and cooks talk about how important the presentation of food is in terms of being pleasing to the eye – the 'visual feast', if you like. So if you're ingesting a colour, you're ingesting a crystallised form of the colour of light that the food you're eating reflects. You can eat to heal your chakras! I have often said that I want to eat red food, or yellow food, for example. This is an expression of my energetic desire to get some input from the light that food reflects. I tend to think of food as colour therapy through stimulating the chakra that resonates with the colour of food that we choose to eat. So, if you have a phase of suddenly wanting to eat 'red' food, the likelihood is that you need to stimulate your root chakra. You can balance the energies of the chakra you want to address by eating food and drinking drinks that are the colour of the chakra you're working with, and you can have great fun by cooking a 'chakra-balanced'

meal or even courses that address each chakra, one at a time. Note that it is difficult to treat the throat chakra (blue) with food – aim for white foods to cool and balance overall.

If you're ingesting a colour, you're ingesting a crystallised form of the colour of light that the food you're eating reflects.

FLOWER REMEDIES

The use of colour in homeopathic medicine is a fairly new concept that has been developed by a number of therapists working in various countries around the world. Having had a great deal of very positive experience in using the Bach flower remedies to help heal both humans and animals, I have been lucky enough to experience the use of remedies prepared from different coloured flowers for myself. These colour flower remedies are far easier to work with to heal yourself than other systems which can cause confusion about which remedy to select. Flower remedies are prepared according to the colour of the bloom, so that it is easy to match the colour of the remedy that the flower is prepared from, to the colour of the chakra or chakras that you're working with. You can even make your own flower essence by picking the blooms of the colour of flower or flowers you want to use, letting them energise in a bowl of spring water (ideally in the sun) for a few hours, then preserving the solution with alchohol – the favoured choice is brandy. You can then add a few drops to water to drink a couple of times a day, or drop them directly on to your tongue. Pick flowers and leaves from plants that you would use in a salad or that are safe to eat (nasturiums, elderflower, roses, herb flowers, violets, and so on). Beware of plants like rhubarb leaves, foxgloves, nightshade, and yew

I have used the remedies on a daily basis as well as for 'rescue'.

that are toxic to humans.

I have used white and green flower remedies (green is prepared from stalk and leaves), to strengthen and balance my crown and heart chakra energies. I was given these essences while making a huge geographical change (moving from one end of the country to another); I was also working hard and undergoing a period of spiritual growth. I used the remedies on a daily basis as well as for 'rescue' – in other words, at times when I suddenly felt like I needed some help! Occasionally they tend to release pent-up emotional energy and initially I can feel weary

or sad, or energetic and excited, but within a few minutes the effect is one of calming, peace and balance, and a renewed commitment and dedication to following my path.

The Bach flower remedies are perhaps the best-known and most widely available off-the-shelf remedy of this type, and there are one or two which seem to correspond to particular chakras, but generally it is safer to dowse for a remedy or use muscle-testing to determine which to use. Bush flower remedies are another essence that I have personal experience of and feel are very useful and effective indeed, particularly if prescribed by an experienced energician or homeopathic practitioner. Flower essences always work on a purely emotional/spiritual level and there is absolutely no harm that can come from using them; if you choose the wrong remedy, you will see no effect at all.

You can blend several Bach flower remedies at a time in spring water for your own remedy and take a few drops on the tongue whenever you feel the need.

HEALING WITH OILS

Aromatherapy is as commonplace today as vitamin supplementation and so essential oils are accessible for everyone. You can buy good-quality essential oils from high-street chains of chemists along with basic

TABLE OF BACH FLOWER REMEDIES FOR DIFFERENT AILMENTS/PERSONALITIES

Agrimony *mental torture behind a brave face*	**Mustard** *deep gloom with no known origin*
Aspen *vague fears of unknown origin*	**Oak** *despondent but struggles on*
Beech *intolerance*	**Olive** *complete exhaustion*
Centaury *weak-willed, subservient*	**Pine** *self-reproach, guilt*
Cerato *seeks advice and confirmation from others*	**Red chestnut** *anxiety for others*
Cherry plum *fear of mind giving way*	**Rock rose** *terror*
Chestnut bud *failure to learn from past mistakes*	**Rock water** *self repression and denial*
Chicory *possessive, selfish*	**Scleranthus** *uncertainty, indecision*
Clematis *dreaminess, lack of interest in present*	**Star of Bethlehem** *shock*
Crab apple *self-hatred, sense of uncleanliness*	**Sweet chestnut** *extreme anguish*
Elm *overwhelmed by responsibility*	**Vervain** *tension, hyperanxiety*
Gentian *discouragement, despondency*	**Vine** *domineering, inflexible*
Gorse *hopelessness, despair*	**Walnut** *protection from change and outside influences*
Heather *self-centredness, self-concern*	**Water violet** *proud, aloof*
Holly *hatred, envy, jealousy*	**White chestnut** *unwanted thoughts, mental arguments*
Honeysuckle *living in the past*	**Wild oat** *uncertainty of correct path in life*
Hornbeam *Monday-morning feeling*	**Wild rose** *resignation, apathy*
Impatiens *impatience*	**Willow** *resentment*
Larch *lack of confidence*	**Rescue remedy** *first aid and emergencies*
Mimulus *fear of known things*	

FLOWER REMEDIES FOR HEALING

I worked with a twenty-six-year-old girl named Rosa who was feeling totally lost and without direction in her life. She was tired of her job, and just seemed to be drifting aimlessly through life with no real enjoyment or satisfaction. She began taking the Bach flower remedy wild oat, which brought about the start of a sequence of dreams where she began to see herself working with children. She had always enjoyed spending time around children but had simply never considered that kind of work as a career option, and she now began to investigate the possibilities. As the changes in her life began to unfold quite dramatically, she started to take a green flower remedy to help her to adjust to all of the sudden shifts that were taking place. Within a very short space of time she was offered a job working as a nanny with a family abroad, thoroughly enjoying the change and the freedom she had been looking for.

guidelines on how to make blends for yourself. Oils contain the energetic vibration of the plant concerned that has been processed into a very concentrated form. Because oils are the essence of a living plant you are working with a deeply powerful energy. Oils also have their own colour which you can use in conjunction with the chakras, though these are often very different than the colours of the original plant from which the oil is extracted. If you like a certain oil, you might find it therapeutic to grow the plant from which it originates, and to use it in cooking, for example. My own personal favourites are lavender, as a relaxing, calming and uplifting oil; helichrysum, which I find deeply soothing; petitgrain, which tends to awaken my spiritual and third-eye energies; marigold, for my skin and for its warm, cheering scent; and lime, for its uplifting and energising qualities.

You can use the chart shown opposite to help select the oils appropriate for your own physical and emotional issues, as well as those appropriate to the chakra or chakras

Oils are much better prepared and used fresh.

you want to work with. You can also dowse or energy-test essential oils when deciding which to use for yourself. Seek specialist advice if you are pregnant as some oils can affect your baby, or if you are prone to allergic skin reactions, have known allergies or an existing skin condition.

Kept away from bright light or dramatic fluctuations in temperature, essential oils can last for quite some time, . Lavender and tea-tree are the only oils that should ever be applied neat to the skin, and this is only ever recommended for healing purposes. Even then, it is safer to mix them with clear aloe-vera jelly, which will also assist in the healing process. The only exception to this is with spike lavender or citronella oils that I routinely dab directly on to my hair or wrists as an insect repellent, but only after the sun has gone down, so as to avoid burning. Generally it is far safer to dilute essential oils at the rate of ten drops to 75 ml of carrier oil; grapeseed oil can be bought very cheaply from most supermarkets, or look for sweet almond or peach kernel oil from specialist shops.

If you are going to use an oil, blend just enough for your immediate use; oils are much better prepared and used fresh. Blends should always be stored in dark glass bottles – I like to find coloured ones to add to the healing effect of the oil. You can also add crystals to the bottle you store your blend in, to add the healing effect of the crystal.

Essential oils can be used therapeutically in many ways. Most people's favourite is with a wonderful

massage from a loving partner, however inexpert; often it is the mere fact that your partner is the one giving the massage that has a healing effect all its own. For any massage, just use a comfortable level of pressure and allow your hands to follow whatever movements feel good to you and your partner. Always pour the oil you are using on to your hands first, to moisten your hands and warm the oil, before applying it

CHAKRA	ASSOCIATED OILS
Crown	Frankincense, neroli, rose
Third Eye	Hyacinth, juniper, lemon, pine, rosemary
Throat	Basil, chamomile, cypress, hyssop, peppermint, petitgrain, rosewood
Heart	Bergamot, geranium, jasmine, lavender, melissa, ylang ylang
Solar Plexus	Black pepper, cardamom, cedarwood, juniper, lime, marjoram
Sacral	Clary sage, fennel, sandalwood, benzoin
Base or Root	Patchouli, thyme, vetiver, myrrh

Plants are living energy therapy; they have scent, colour, and a frequency of vibration all of their own.

to the skin. Feet, hands, and the head are worth special attention; according to aromatherapists the therapeutic effect of any essential oil is more rapidly felt if applied to the soles of the feet.

Another way of using essential oils is to add drops into water in a vaporiser or oil burner to create a healing atmosphere at home, to balance your energies, relax, revitalise, or address a particular issue. I have a friend who burns drops of rose, geranium and clary sage to help combat her symptoms of premenstrual tension. You can also dab drops of oil on to a handkerchief to carry with you throughout the day, add them to your bath, or even add a few drops to some water in a

spray bottle and use as a body spray.

Plants are living energy therapy; they have scent, colour, and a frequency of vibration all of their own, far clearer, purer and higher than ours (hence the health-giving benefits of a vegetarian diet!). Because the energy of plants is so uplifting and therapeutic, gardening can be wonderful – a therapy that blends coloured light therapy, aromatherapy and straight plant energy therapy. So if you're not a gardener, spending some time in this soothing and creative activity is worth a try. People find their own style of gardening – I, for one, love masses of colour and a riot of old-fashioned flowers. You can even plant swathes of colour to balance your chakras – a real healing garden!

THE ENERGY OF CRYSTALS

The healing effect of natural sources of energy is the principle behind crystal healing. Stones have the same basic sub-atomic conscious energy that all matter has, and the wonderful healing properties of crystals have to be personally experienced in order to be fully understood. Crystals of course can be used in groups of colour appropriate to the chakra or chakras you want to work with. As with all the other remedies, dowse or muscle-test to choose your crystal, or just pick one that appeals to you.

There are numerous ways of using crystals therapeutically; they do not even have to be touching your skin to help to move and release your energy. You can place your chosen crystal on your desk at work, near your bed at home, or in the room you spend a lot of time in. You can wear crystals as jewellery (most of us do in some form or another), carry them in your pocket, and you can even soak them in spring water to make a spray for use on your body or around your home.

When choosing a crystal, pick one that looks bright. Any stone that looks dull or tired may have been handled a great deal before you buy it and could be carrying other people's energetic residues. Most crystals can be cleaned by being soaked in spring water or run under a tap, but if you have a stone that seems soft or crumbly avoid getting it wet. Clean it by leaving it on the windowsill in the sun for a day.

As I mentioned at the start of this chapter, all vibrational medicine is simply a range of tools used to harness your healing intent – a little like bringing in the heavy artillery. Tools are the way to open your energy body and conscious being to new vibrations of energy and thus, to release held patterns, raise awareness

CHAKRA	ASSOCIATED STONES
Crown	Amethyst, sugilite, diamond, fluorite, clear and rutilated quartz
Third Eye	Lapis lazuli, sodalite, purple fluorite, sapphire, azurite, amethyst
Throat	Aquamarine, turquoise, blue topaz, blue lace agate, blue calcite
Heart	Rose quartz, emerald, green tourmaline, chrysophrase, green calcite, aventurine, rhodochrosite
Solar Plexus	Topaz, citrine, amber, tiger's eye
Sacral	Carnelian, orange calcite, orange jasper
Base or Root	Garnet, ruby, coral, haematite, obsidian

and promote healing. The next stage in healing work is to focus purely on the energy of intent. The strongest and most straightforward form of healing is in the power of your intent through hands-on healing, meditation and visualisation, which we will examine in the next chapter.

In the last chapter we looked at some of the tools of
energy medicine that can help you to begin to let go of
any established patterns that you feel are holding you back
or preventing you from living life in a healed and whole
way. Hopefully you will have found some ways to help
yourself feel at peace, and may perhaps have gone through

CHAPTER 5

Contact

a process of letting go of some of the held energy that
was no longer helpful to you. Your releases may have taken
place on a physical, emotional or mental level, and you are
likely to find that spiritually you have grown through the
experience. You may feel more in touch with the essence
of who you really are. It may even be that some of the
energy medicines will have helped to centre you to the
point of finding you own inner experience of peace and
wellbeing; the centre where your soul is at ease. If so, you
will have shifted your state of being just a little.

TO BE AT PEACE

As I have said before, the point about all healing is not that you are trying to 'get' somewhere or to achieve some kind of perfect spiritual state so that your life is always happy. All you're aiming to do, is just to let go and Be. Think of it as letting go, doing nothing, stopping trying, or whatever you find is the

most accessible way to achieve a sense of the most peaceful, whole, wellness. This state of peace is actually available to all of us at any time, because it is how we all are, within our innermost sense of soul. In this chapter, I'm going to give you some ways to access the peace within your soul energy which will help you let go of all the conditioning, clutter and 'stuff' that you hold on to preventing you from

feeling that sense of inner peace.

Ultimately, the peace of your soul energy is where the true healing is, because it is from there that we learn to find one of two ways that can bring about a permanent and profound shift in our lives and enable long-term healing. The first way is to gain the strength to know that we are ultimately all-powerful within our own lives. We create our own reality with every moment of every day. If honouring our integrity means we do need to change something in our lives, then we can at any moment if we really want to. This is the kind of simple truth that is all-empowering, but that so many people forget much of the time. You don't have to do that job; you don't have to live in that house; you don't have to stay in that relationship – you have a choice.

Of course, this means letting go of a lot of our own sense of victimhood and oppression, which brings about a huge healing in itself. I recently spent a couple of days with a friend who came to stay with me because she was feeling utterly miserable in her job and her home life. She felt used and trapped, and in desperate need of some time and space to herself. She felt totally dictated to in her job, and unable to make a difference to people who are suffering a basic infringement of their rights as human beings. At home, she lives with four males (her father, her husband and her two sons) all of whom, she feels, treat her as a personal resource for money, housework, attention, and general nurturing, without making any contribution to her in return. She was at the point of feeling that she wanted to leave her whole life, close the door and not look back, and so she dropped some clothes into a bag and came to stay for a couple of days. She wanted to know how she would feel out of the situation, and at the same time, to consider other ways of living. Having walked away from her house, her family, her pets and her job – just for a couple of days – the sense of power she was feeling was incredible. Together, we looked at a community for her to live and work in which seemed idyllic – a wonderful location, a totally different way of working, a group of like-minded people, and a spiritual ethic with which she identified deeply. However, while this community could have been the answer for her, spending time there gave her the space to see that although she could walk away from her life on a permanent basis and indeed, had the power to do so at any moment, she did actually want to be with her family at home. There are some things she will need to change, and the very strength she needs to

change them is the same strength that enabled her to walk out of the door and say, 'I'm off'. She is not a victim of her life, but the person who is creating it, and she can say, 'I'm not going to do that any more'. For her, that means not behaving as a resource for her family without expecting something in return, and it also means that she will 's change her job. With all that set to change, her urge to run away has left her.

CHANGE AND ACCEPTANCE

My friend is a perfect example of how each of us can find the strength and clarity to make a change. She listened to her soul and said, 'I can be different'. However, the peace and depth that she found within her own

If honouring our integrity means we do need to change something in our lives, then we can at any moment if we really want to.

soul energy have also given her the ability to heal herself in the second important way that comes from working at soul level – to accept that some things are actually fine. There are elements of her life that she has decided simply to accept and not keep fighting because actually, there is nothing that she needs to do. For example, she doesn't need to leave her husband because there is

Acceptance in its purest sense means accepting yourself for what and who you are.

entrapped. It's rising above the level of the ego to the level of the higher self or soul and resting in the knowledge that everything is really fine just as it is and that there is no need to keep pumping energy into struggle and conflict. Acceptance in its purest sense means accepting yourself for what and who you are, and honouring yourself as you are, instead of constantly fighting with your essence, trying to improve yourself, or do something differently. It means realising that where you are is the right place for you, and engaging in your life to the point where it feels right to be doing what you do. It's about putting your heart and soul into a situation, instead of withdrawing from it.

A big part of the process of acceptance is what some spiritual teachers would call 'surrender', because it is a releasing of personal will at a superficial level about what is happening in your life. It's about accepting that there is an order to the universe and a synchronicity that is far deeper and greater than anything we could wish to understand. It means that we move through the process of releasing on many different levels. These might include releasing the need to do something about events, situations or processes in your life; or releasing your judgement about whether a given event or process is

nothing wrong with her marriage. From our essential soul energy, we can find the grace to accept some things the way they are, and stop chewing away at ourselves and our lives (which is the kind of inner conflict that brings about emotional and physical sickness).

Acceptance is not a state of apathy; it has nothing to do with letting things wash over you – it just means that all the turmoil, analysing, inner nagging, and angst are released. True acceptance is a state of rising above all the minor and superficial elements of our lives in which we allow ourselves to become 'right' or 'wrong'; or releasing the need to make decisions about your life, and in fact, releasing all ego-level involvement with any of the processes that occur around you. This process also involves releasing your past, as well, including your mental/emotional baggage, thus bringing about a deep shift within your own perspective. Acceptance is also about learning to see things not from the level of defence and ego and judgement and blame, but from the level where you have a deep sense of inner knowing that whatever happens is ultimately perfect. This process of acceptance is partly what my friend has gone through in going home and deciding that she is living in the right place by being with her family. She has accepted that perhaps she is experiencing and learning exactly what she needs to, by staying right where she is – that she doesn't actually need to run away at all.

At first it sounds like a tall order to 'let go' to the point of not going through an intellectual trauma about every little occurrence in your life; and particularly, about some of the bigger occurrences. Similarly, it might seem difficult to let go of all your current beliefs about your need to be in a job, have a certain income, live in a certain house, and that you could change your entire reality at any given moment. There are no hard and fast rules about when to accept and when to disengage, because no two people or situations are the same; even the same situation can have different implications for two different people. What is important is understanding that while you don't have to be a victim, you don't have to struggle either, and knowing which path to take.

And this brings you to the simplest and most gentle state of being that there is – the state of being from which your soul agenda truly comes forth into your physical life. By opening up to your deepest inner guidance and sense of your truest self, you will begin to see when you need to act, and when to let things be. You do not need to make specific plans, achieve any targets or even make decisions. Just 'being' in the moment is the process of engaging fully with life on a soul level and living from your whole sense of self with no conflict, no worry, and no sickness. This simple sense of 'being' is where feeling healed is a way of life. Some of us need a little help to get there, though, so, let's look at some ways in which you can access your soul energy to find the peace that will enable you to let go.

TOUCHING YOUR SOUL

There is no set way in which you learn to reach your soul energy. There are many ways, and any or all of them – meditation, yoga, a healing treatment, or taking a long, relaxing bath – might work for you. For some people walking the dog, going for a drive, painting a picture, or pottering in the garden might do it. Try some of the suggestions I'm offering here and see what works best for you, but remember all the while that this is not work or a struggle, and you're not trying to attain some incredible state of healed bliss. This is just an exploration – a little walk around your own awareness to find a quiet place to be, so enjoy it.

The easier it is for you to access your sense of inner strength, gentleness and peace, the easier you will find it to maintain that centre of connection with the creative, healing energy from which your soul 'comes'. You're actually just letting go of all the clutter and conditioning which keeps you in a lower state of awareness, to be at the level where your truest sense of being is; the level of unlimited creative energy with which you are able to experience life. You're reaching back to the point at which you are simply conscious energy with a drive to have a physical experience and to know what life is. Remember also that this energy is healing; it is the energy of creation, of love, of the quantum light/matter of the unified field. This energy is also utterly healed; in other words, it is perfect! One of the most calming, uplifting and empowering thoughts to have is that you are a perfect soul. All you need to do to experience that perfection is to let go of all the ego-level junk that keeps you from experiencing that state of peaceful perfection.

The first and most important step in reaching your soul energy is to place your intent in that thought. Sometimes, in fact, that's all you need. So, state your intent to yourself in any way that is simple, clear, and concise. Write down a phrase that sums up your intent perfectly, because in future, whenever you feel the need to reach into your soul, to be in that peace and strength, you can refer to your key phrase to take you there. It's not necessary to have a long or complicated affirmation; a few words that clearly state the place where you want your awareness to be are

all it will take. Phrases using 'I am' are very creative and have a deep sense of dynamic, quiet energy about them. For example, your phrase could be, 'I am at peace', or 'I am soul', 'I am centred', or 'I am whole'. Try them out and see what you are most comfortable with. 'I am' is also a way of reminding yourself that you are not trying to create a state of mind or get somewhere; that there is a level of you which is already there. Once you have stated your intent, keep your phrase in your mind whenever you begin a soul-meeting exercise, or whenever you feel the need to access your soul energy.

MEDITATION – HOW TO DO NOTHING

One of the easiest ways in which to reach your soul energy is through meditation. Many people believe that there are all kinds of stages, techniques, and trappings involved in

The easier it is for you to access your sense of inner strength, gentleness and peace, the easier you will find it to maintain that centre of connection.

meditation, but it's really just a big word for doing nothing. Meditation is nothing more complicated than the process of being at peace. Rather than being an activity, or something you do, it's actually something you don't do, and the less effort involved, the better. You don't need any tools for meditating, either, and while there are all kinds of musical recordings and even spoken tapes and CDs that will guide you through meditation and relaxation, you can end up more caught up in following the meditation than in actually relaxing, thus missing the whole point of the process. I have a friend who once attended a guided meditation session. She was so concerned with projecting a pink mist of love and seeing a golden ball of light and following it through the clouds to a crystal castle, that she felt quite exhausted afterwards! If a little soft music helps you to relax, and stops your mind focusing on outside noises such as traffic or the refrigerator, then use it. Equally, if you're happy just in a peaceful room with no sound, that's fine too. I tend to have my ten or twenty minutes in silence, since for me, there is a level of effort involved in hearing the sound of music that I'd rather be free of; aside from which, if you have really shifted your awareness to a point of soul energy, you'll be quite unaware of the music or any other sound anyway.

So, all you need to do is to wear comfortable clothing and find a place where you will be undisturbed for ten or twenty minutes. Good posture is conducive to a free flow of energy through your body, and energy can move through your body more freely if you sit in a relaxed but upright position, with your feet on the floor. However, I know that some people find that easier than others and if you want to sit in an easy chair or lay on the floor, that's fine. Lying down, flat on your back is actually better for you in energetic terms than sitting slouched or in even the slightest pain, so just do whatever comes naturally.

Make sure that the temperature is comfortable for you. Because your body tends to slow down during meditation, you can feel cooler than you normally would, so you might even like to cover yourself with a blanket or put on a pair of socks. I quite often just get into bed and lie down. Strictly disciplined students of meditation would probably not advocate lying down in case you fall asleep, but my belief is that if you need to sleep, you should sleep. One school of Buddhism actually teaches a lying-down meditation, so meditating on your back may be something worth spending some time exploring. There is nothing about soul-level healing which says you will never feel physically tired again, and if you are struggling to stay awake, you're not going to relax, so go with what feels good for you.

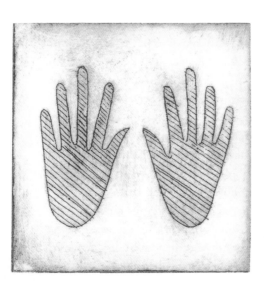

With all the physical considerations dealt with, just take a few deep breaths – not forced, just whole breaths. Close your eyes and relax. Gently state or repeat to yourself your phrase of intent to place your awareness at soul level, if you want to. Then, simply let go. If you find that thoughts are drifting through your mind, that's fine; don't go with them or focus on them, just let them drift through and gently bring your awareness back to the point of relaxation. If it helps, use your phrase to bring yourself back to your intention. All you are doing is letting your mind rest. Don't try and do anything; trying to be still is the hardest thing in the world and would actually block any useful insights that come to you anyway. Let your awareness drift to a place of peace and rest.

Sometimes, I do actually suggest to people that when first learning to meditate, they prepare for sleep. That zone where you are neither asleep nor awake is the point at which you are in your deepest level of energetic awareness. As you begin to relax, go with the peace and remain there for as long as you like. You're not trying to achieve anything other than a deep sense of peace, so just go with it and see where it takes you. As and when you begin to come round, or lift your awareness to a more conscious level, gently

become aware of your body; wiggle your fingers, take a few deep breaths (if you're sitting with your feet on the ground, wiggle your toes), and slowly open your eyes. Generally when you 'come to' you will feel at ease, revitalised, far more peaceful and often more aware than before.

Sometimes you might come back with thoughts, ideas, or even a dream-like sequence that will be useful to you during the course of the day, or relevant to some aspect of your healing process or life at the moment.

If you can remain still, relaxed and undisturbed for ten minutes, that's fine. If you can get twenty minutes, so much the better. The ideal is to allow yourself that meditating space for around twenty minutes every day, and maybe even twice a day at weekends. In reality, however, in a busy household it's just not always possible to find the time or space to meditate, so even two minutes is better than nothing! Do persist, and just keep creating the space and

The ideal is to allow yourself that meditating space for around twenty minutes every day, and maybe even twice a day at weekends.

stillness in your life. With time and practice, you will be able to state your phrase, close your eyes for a few moments and take a deep breath to find the same sense of tranquillity as you do during meditation. I have found that at times I can sigh, or just take a single deep breath to find that centred soul energy and regain the sense of dynamic stillness that I

need to get through whatever is happening around me. So whether you're behind your desk, in the supermarket, or even walking down the street, a single deep breath can bring you back to your centre.

Meditation is a powerful and uplifting tool for letting go of your worries, so if something is troubling you, meditation could help you to resolve the situation. You can take the problem into the meditation with you and offer it up to the universe to handle; this is a little like saying, 'Thy will be done'. My own personal stock phrase is 'whatever!', meaning not that I couldn't care less, but that 'Whatever needs to happen will happen, I don't need to fret or do anything about this. I can just trust.' You can also ask your question to your higher self or inner guidance as you go into a meditation in the hope of gaining some kind of answer to your issue. Sometimes, you'll come out with an answer; other times, you might just bring worry and a sense of looking for the answer or waiting for something to happen into your peaceful relaxation time, so it can be easier to leave it aside. You may gain thoughts or impulses from meditation. It is often a positive thing to go and do whatever it is that has inspired you, which is why I call meditation 'the eureka state'. Use your judgement; don't feel that you must chase ego wanderings – like a sudden urge to do the washing up, for example – but if you have a profound insight, go with it. You can see, also, why I say that you will find your own way to reach that inner depth of soul energy. You might feel that sense of

still strength while doing something very mundane with your body; like walking, for example; so if you meditate best when you're walking, forget the comfy chair, just go for a walk (but keep your eyes open!). I find a great sense of peace when riding my horses and I know people who meditate their way round golf courses, so there are no hard and fast rules.

VISUALISATION – MEETING YOUR SELF

Activity and meditation can go together, if you handle them carefully, even though you are

reaching for a sense of stillness and peace. If you find it hard to let go when sitting still and doing absolutely nothing, a visualisation might help you to relax. Go through exactly the same process as you would to meditate, only instead of

Go through exactly the same process as you would to meditate, only instead of letting your mind drift to find a still place, take a more active part in the process.

letting your mind drift to find a still place, take a more active part in the process and use your imagination to find your soul energy. You can actually go through a little meditating journey to meet your soul. As you close your eyes, do so with the intent that you are going to meet your soul. Then, as you begin to relax, think of a place that is perhaps somewhere you enjoy going and where you feel relaxed – a still or peaceful place; somewhere you feel safe and happy. It can be real or imaginary; I have a kind of imaginary hillside stone circle that I go to where, because it is imaginary, there are no other people to make noises or blunder in on me!

As you begin your meditation then, let your awareness go to 'your' place; imagine you are there. Take some time to see the place around you on all sides, and look up at the sky (or roof, if you are in a building), down at the ground (or floor), and see the colours of the scenery around you. Hear any sounds, like the music of the birds singing, the movement of the wind, or water trickling in a stream. Smell any scents, like grass, soil, flowers, or just the air around you. Feel the sun on your face or body, or the wind in your hair. Take a few minutes to immerse yourself completely in the place. Then, ask to meet your soul. See or imagine yourself sitting or standing a little way away and walk towards where you are. Look at

Sit down with yourself for a while and just see yourself relaxing; looking around at where you are, watching the wind in the trees, the birds flying overhead.

yourself as if you are looking in the mirror; your face, your body, the clothes you tend to wear, the way you smile. Sit down with yourself for a while and just see yourself relaxing; looking around at where you are, watching the wind in the trees, the birds flying overhead, the movement of the clouds, or whatever is in your particular place. If you want to, you can ask yourself

a question; this can either be in the present tense – 'Should I move house?' – or past tense if the event has already happened. For example, before I moved house I recently asked myself, 'Did you go?', and the answer was yes. This is a wonderful technique for dealing with issues if you are in a real quandary. In point of fact, you are actually communicating with your own deepest level of awareness, so it is a deeply powerful process.

Once you have spent some time with yourself just being at peace, then slowly bring your awareness back into your physical body in the present, to the place where you're meditating on a physical level. Feel the atmosphere of the room around you; become aware of any sounds you can hear; wiggle your toes and fingers, take a few deep breaths, and, when you feel ready, gently open your eyes. Coming back from a visualisation can take a little time as you gradually bring your awareness back to the physical plane, so don't rush the process. Stay with it for as long as you feel you want to and just enjoy the feeling of tranquil ease. Afterwards you will feel deeply relaxed and refreshed, and probably energised on many different levels. Again, with practice, you will learn to take a deep breath and a long blink to see yourself back in that peaceful place of knowing and happiness, at any time during a hectic or trying day.

The more often you return to your soul energy, or bring your feeling of centredness into your everyday physical life, the more you will begin to feel, think, and operate from a level of soul-consciousness. You can also use visualisation to access your soul energy for any form of healing work. So, if you're unwell, for example, you can go to your peaceful place and meet yourself looking well and healthy, to bring that sense of perfect peace and health into your conscious mind and your intention to be well. If you suffer an injury, you can journey inside your body and see your tissues rebuilding themselves at a cellular level. A popular method used by people with growths or tumours is to see their growth falling to pieces or melting away to nothing. You can see yourself in any way you choose to – slim, if you want to lose weight, receiving your pass marks if you're taking an exam, being paid if you are owed some money, and so on. All you're doing is harnessing the deepest and most dynamic creative energy of your own soul.

LEARNING TO HEAL HANDS-ON

A deeply empowering way in which to raise your own level of awareness and learn to work from your soul energy is to do some hands-on

healing work yourself. Disciplines like Reiki were in fact originally intended as a means of personal spiritual work, rather than a therapy for treating others, though that is an endlessly useful sideline. Reiki is a well-known Japanese healing and relaxation therapy that is readily available to most people in many countries throughout the West. The ability to work with hands-on energy is passed to you through the teacher in a process known as 'attunement', which is a way of tuning your own energy field into the universal energy that is all around us. Over a period, Reiki attunements will help to raise your level of awareness to one of a centred, peaceful strength.

Once you have mastered a skill like working with hands-on energy, you can place your hands on your own body at any time of the day, and anywhere, to give yourself an immediate reconnection to the deeply creative, healing energy of which we are all a part. It is instantly relaxing and will serve to recharge

and revitalise your own energy within a very short space of time, as well as to relieve pain and speed up your body's natural healing processes. This is a perfect way to help clear your mind and energy field of any clutter that accumulates during the course of the day. Aside from treating yourself for any physical or emotional disturbances you might experience, the more regularly you give yourself a blast of healing energy, the clearer and stronger your energy will become, and the more you will find

yourself able to remain centred. Of course, it is also a useful tool for healing and relaxing other members of your family, your friends, and your pets.

During the attunement process itself, your connection with soul-level creative energy is deeply strengthened to the point where you can project energy out through the chakras in the palms of your hands and at the ends of your fingertips. The connection you receive works with your own soul energy so that in time, you find yourself maintaining the feeling of peace and centred energy, and the level of awareness that you are in at soul level, more and more. As you work with the energy itself it also helps to bring your mind to a level of deeply peaceful consciousness so that even if you are helping to treat other people, you will still be benefiting on some level from the energy working through you. The energy you work with actually helps to lift some of the natural energy pool (sometimes called 'kundalini' energy) that lies in the area of the root chakra, as well as strengthening the flow of energy inwards and down through your crown chakra to the earth. So as you become more aware and centred, you also become more able to function in a spiritual way or from a soul level while maintaining your connection with the grounded nature of a physical existence. Self-healing is something everyone should learn and there are many healing teachers now working in a totally ethical way to keep the cost of attuning as low as possible rather than making it into a profit-oriented business. It would be a great help to the human race in general if there were someone in every street (if not every house!) that you could just call on for a quick attunement. Just think how this would help to strengthen your soul-level connection and with what ease you would be able to shift your awareness to that wonderful, tranquil energy!

EMPOWERMENT FOR HEALING ENERGY

During meditation you can perform visualisations to help in strengthening that energetic connection for yourself, and anyone who is already working with energy can perform a quick healing empowerment on anyone else to give them the ability to channel energy for themselves. This is not a Reiki attunement but it is a reliable and incredibly powerful ritual that enables you to begin to connect with our source energy and channel it, strengthening your own connection and enabling you to help others at the same time. This empowerment process is actually a Buddhist technique. It can be performed by anyone for anyone, and once you have learned how to do it, you can give an empowerment to anyone who has a few minutes to spare for healing and relaxation. This empowerment for soul-level energy connection is a clear and simple method that gives the recipient the energy that they personally need to receive. That energy will work through them to raise their own awareness and ability to centre, as well as having the wonderful side-effect of giving them the ability to project energy through their hands to help others to relax, to strengthen their own soul-level

During the attunement process, your connection with soul-level creative energy is deeply strengthened.

energy connection, and to heal. Try this, even if you have never worked hands-on with healing or energy of any kind. If, on the other hand, you are already working with an energy connection of some kind, try giving this empowerment to others. All hands-on work is basically the same process; it's only the way that people explain or understand it that varies. Just go through the process with the intent that both you and the recipient gain a connection to source energy; if it's right for you, it will work.

Visualise a column of white light between your hands and slowly draw your hands down the whole length of the person's body.

To give an empowerment for self-healing, sit the recipient in a chair, or on the floor with their eyes gently closed and hands together. Stand in front of them. With your palms together above their head, allow the energy to come through your hands, (or for those of you who have never worked with energy before, just visualise a healing energy flowing from your hands). Visualise a column of white light between your hands and slowly draw your hands down the whole length of the person's body, to the ground, drawing the light with them.

Next, place one hand above the other over the person's crown (not touching the body) and offer some energy. Then (really just when you feel you should) move your hands to either side of the head and again give a blast of energy. Then, again offer energy at the brow chakra (hands with thumbs and first fingertips together in triangle, fingers flat together), and then with the same hand-shape again project energy at the fingertips. Continue to draw the light energy all the way down to the ground again. Finally, sweep your hands and the light all the way up the front of the body to finish at the head.

If you perform empowerment technique a few times, the recipient will begin to feel the characteristic tingling in the hands that is symptomatic of healing energy coming through from the crown chakra, down and out through the palms and fingertips. During the process itself, they are likely to become deeply relaxed and in touch with their own soul energy. Empowerment is intensely peaceful, energising and relaxing, so the more regularly you can practise with your partner, friends and family, the more you will strengthen your own healing and clarity. Empowerment can be used to help people and animals who are ill to strengthen their own energetic connection (for animals, just offer energy to the feet or even the nose at the stage where you offer humans energy to the hands). Even if, as I say, you have never worked with healing energy at all, do try this empowerment process – it works! After three or four repeats you will begin to feel the flow of energy coming through your hands. Once the flow has begun, it will stay with you for life and will strengthen the more you use it.

You can also give yourself an empowerment with your own hands. Sit with your hands folded for a few moments at the point where you would have been projecting energy at the recipient's hands. If you can find a few moments during the course of the day (it only takes a couple of minutes) to sit in a quiet place and self-empower, you are instantly reconnecting your centre and deepening your awareness. Just as importantly, you will be helping to clear your own energy of anything you don't need. Self-empowering is a great way to release anything that is no longer useful to you and it can bring about a powerful release process. The energy will reach whatever level of your own energy field that it needs to work at; all you're doing is recharging your batteries, so you might find that you go through a release on a physical,

mental, or emotional level after you receive empowerments and also through giving them. I used to break out in spots when I did a number of empowerments for myself and others, for example when I was giving workshops. It was a bit of a joke between my husband and I that the first day's students were the only ones who took me seriously. On subsequent days I was so spotty as a result of the clearance process, that people looked at me as if to say, 'How can you expect to tell us anything about healing, when you

look as though you need some yourself!' Of course, by giving empowerments I am healing myself on an ongoing basis – and going through the resultant releases afterwards! The process actually works through you so you receive the energy yourself as you offer it to others.

Remember that there is a consciousness and intelligence behind the whole process of working with energy that goes far deeper than anything we could choose for ourselves. So, there is nothing you can do wrong and it's not down to you to decide how the process works for the recipient of the empowerment or even for yourself. The energy will do whatever it needs to do.

SHARING EMPOWERMENTS AND HEALING WITH OTHERS

Self-empowering can be useful and helpful, but there is nothing so wonderful as receiving empowerments or healing treatments from others so that you can reach your deep state of peaceful soul energy and relaxation. This is what helps to stimulate healing on a physical level so the more you relax, the better, which is of course easier if someone else is treating you. Sharing an empowerment with each other at the start or end of the day is also a profoundly peaceful and relaxing way to centre yourself and your partner. If you can swap healing massages or just a short hands-on treatment in a chair with your partner or a friend, you should feel the benefits of re-establishing your connection with your soul-level energy. You can give anyone a short ten- or twenty-minute treatment in a chair or even sitting on the ground, in your lunch break at the office, at school, or in the middle of a football field!

Make sure that you allow yourself a little time undisturbed by the telephone or by other people, and a place that is comfortable and warm enough to relax – in summer I often give people treatments outside in the garden.

For a more relaxing treatment, have the recipient lie down in a place where it's comfortable for you to work round them. Again, make sure that you're going to remain undisturbed for a while; if it helps you both to relax, play some soft music or dim the lights a little. Then, offer energy first at the shoulders and head, and work all the way round the body, including the centre of the body, hips, knees and feet, and then up again to the top (from the opposite side to the one you went down, if possible). Finish at the shoulders. It's easy to spend forty minutes or so treating in this way because both giver and recipient tend to drop into a deep state of relaxation. Give yourselves a little time afterwards to come round – or, ideally, you can do this before bed! Working with each other in this way is not just a method for healing, it's also a tool for centring and bringing your awareness at soul level into a more conscious way of living.

Of course, if you choose not to self-treat, a professional healing therapist can provide the same benefits, whether they use hands-on healing, or other forms of energy work like zero-balancing, cranial osteopathy or cranio-sacral therapy. However, the more you learn to strengthen your own energetic connection for yourself, the more you will find yourself able to let go and simply bring your awareness at soul level into your everyday way of living for deep and true long-term healing.

GIVING A HEALING MASSAGE

1 To give a short treatment, ask the recipient to close their eyes as it will help them to relax and centre.

2 Place your hands and offer energy for a few minutes at a time on the shoulders, head, either side of the chest/back, the centre of the body, the knees and feet, finishing at the shoulders again.

3 Afterwards, ask them to take a few deep breaths and gently open their eyes when they feel ready to do so.

Remember that even a short treatment can be very relaxing and centring, and that some people may need a few moments to gather themselves before continuing with the day's activities.

Now that you have learned to access your soul energy, we are going to look at some ways in which to utilise it to bring a positive and peaceful influence into your life. Once you begin to return to your centre on an ongoing basis, you will find that you are living at the level of the energy of your soul. It is worth taking a little time, each and every day, on as regular a basis as you can, to just stop, and let your awareness return to the level of your soul energy. It

CHAPTER 6

Enlightenment

may help to give yourself a little hands-on energy, perhaps to your heart, to help you to reach that sense of peace. The more you do this, the more you will be able to maintain that connection and centre of energy; and the more you will find yourself letting go. So, having learned how to shift your sense of awareness and energy to the level of your soul, let's look at some ways in which you can maintain the momentum of that shift.

LIVING FROM YOUR SOUL

Letting your soul shine through is the greatest part of the process of enlightenment. What you're actually doing is functioning from the level of your soul energy, and using that energy to change the way in which you live. The word 'enlightenment' literally means, 'to let the light in' and the more you allow yourself to be in

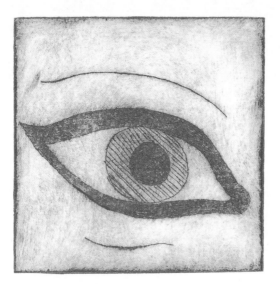

that perfect place of light energy, the more you are living in an enlightened way. Living from the level of your soul will also bring about a profound sense that you are being, or perhaps experiencing your world, in a whole new way. Because you are spending more and more time functioning from a higher level of awareness, the experiences you perceive and the way in which you feel that your life is unfolding will change for the better

in every way. It is almost as though you are seeing the world through the eyes of your soul and it may surprise and delight you to find that your world can look so different from the way it did before.

Living your life with a sense of grace and wholeness is simply a matter of maintaining the momentum of the shift you have made. It's not about work, but it does involve a willingness to move and grow with the flow of energy that is moving through your life. There are all kinds of ways that you can use your energy to work positively in your life and to maintain the momentum of your healing and growth. Intent is the most powerful way to place your energy in your own life and to help add positive influence to your experiences and wellbeing. Your intent to keep 'on flow' is an important and integral part of your long-term healing. The fact is that by this time, even if you decide that the whole thing is a load of baloney, you will have dipped your toe in the water for long enough to make a ripple, and that ripple will undulate through your life!

ENERGISING WITH INTENT

Intent is not something you need to work hard at; you just have to be aware of what your true intent is. Reaffirming your intention to continue to let go and be at peace is a way of energising that feeling throughout each day. This in itself is enough to add energy to the process of healing in your life. I have often had students or clients who take their own healing so very seriously that they get somewhat bogged down in the necessity to keep seeing themselves shifting and releasing and growing and raising their level of awareness. People's egos can very easily latch on to the idea that, for example, if they don't meditate often 'enough' or for long 'enough', they won't grow 'enough'. As I always say, 'Let go.' There is no right or wrong with energy; there is only what is appropriate for you. Of course, the more time you spend in a state of relaxed and peaceful being, the more you will feel centred and energised and able to energise your life from your soul energy. But it is also necessary to live a physical, practical existence, or, as the Zen saying goes, 'chop wood, carry water,' the point being that sometimes you just engage in living your life, instead of being concerned with how you are living it, what your level of awareness is, how you're perceiving what you perceive, what it all means, and so on.

GROWING THE POSITIVE ENERGY

Once you start to consciously reaffirm and engage your intent in the way you live, and then just allow that process to continue to work, your intent will gather more energy of itself. This is how you can work with the process of using energy to attract more positive energy to itself, in the same way as using a more positive expression of language (as I mentioned in chapter three) can draw more positive energy to your experience. This is a wonderful example of how we can all experience, on a practical level, our basic energetic interconnection with all life. It's an amazing phenomenon but at the same time an utterly natural one. This is not to say that once you have decided to release your held patterns, you can stop

As I always say, 'Let go.' There is no right or wrong with energy; there is only what is appropriate for you.

being concerned about your healing, or just give up and forget about it. It's only that it's necessary to realise that you do not have to continually slog away and take it all so terribly seriously. Once you have taken the first steps, the energy with which you have begun to work will attract more of the same energy to itself. The process will continue to work for you, so long as it is your intent that you are willing for it to do so.

One of the ways in which you will experience the energy of your own

intent attracting more energy to itself is in noticing more of what some people would call happy coincidences, or what Jung called

You can begin to see the world as working for you in a very beautiful, ordered and naturally harmonious way.

synchronicity, as I mentioned in chapter two. I'll explain more about this in the next chapter, when we'll look at the synchronicity of your life on a practical level and how you can work with it now and in the future rather than understanding it retrospectively.

Synchronicity is a phenomenon whereby whatever you need to come in to your life comes; and whatever you need to let go of leaves your life without struggle, conflict, or drama. Some people call this process

'manifesting', because by placing the energy of your intent upon something, it is possible to attract it into your life. You can begin to see the world as working for you in a very beautiful, ordered and naturally harmonious way, instead of seeing it as being full of obstacles, problems, and stumbling blocks. To give you an example of how synchronicity works, some time ago I ordered a book from my local shop. Usually, within a week of my ordering a book, the bookseller telephones me to say that it has arrived and I have to make a journey to collect it. In this instance, about three weeks after ordering the book, I happened to be in the town where the bookshop is, and realised that I hadn't had a message to say it had arrived. So, I called into the shop and said to the bookseller, 'Hi, David, has my book come in yet?' He shook his head. 'No, it's not in. I don't know why. I'll chase it up for you, shall I?' At that second, a delivery man walked through the door carrying a box with a publisher's name on it. David's mouth dropped open. 'Clare,' he said, 'this is your book!'

This kind of thing happens to me all the time. I might need a parking space outside a printing shop so that I can get course notes copied for a workshop, and as I drive towards the shop, a car pulls out to leave me a space. Or, just when a bill needs paying someone telephones and asks me to teach a workshop or give a talk, so the money to pay the bill is there. I might be thinking about a friend who I haven't spoken to for a while, and just then she sends me an e-mail. Or, I might be thinking about how useful it would be to have a simple technique that I could pass on to other people for their own healing, and someone invites me to learn how to give empowerments. It's not that I'm living a charmed life – I do get the occasional tyre puncture, or one of my horses goes lame (usually because I haven't been aware of the signs that life was showing me). But mostly, I do live in a state of magical being in which my life is more blessed than I could ever have asked for it to be, and which makes the world look utterly gorgeous to me.

THE POWER OF SHIFTING PERSPECTIVE

So, working from the level of your Of course, seeing the world in this way attracts more of the same wonderful energy into my life. The more you project positive energy, the more positive energy you attract back into your life. Those synchronicities are so obvious and so clearly working in my favour that I can honestly say that I feel my interconnection with the rest of life. Perhaps this is where the saying, 'Be careful of what you wish for, it may come true,' comes from. By thinking a thought, the

consciousness of creative energy is affected to the point where the thought gains the energetic momentum with which to fulfil itself. Seeing the world from this level of awareness and engaging in the process in a positive way is also about closing the gap between your unconscious thoughts and feelings,

and your conscious existence. By letting the energy of your soul shine through, your unconscious needs or feelings become conscious, energised intentions that have the strength to attract the outcome to themselves. This is what I tend to think of as actually living from your essential energy; of giving your soul agenda free play in the real world and letting it lead you through life. It's the process of bringing your soul agenda into physicality.

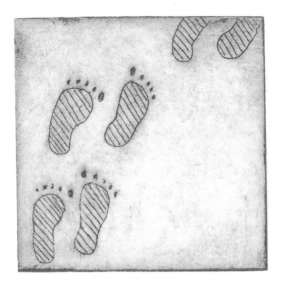

Of course, living at this level of awareness can bring enormous opportunities to shift some of your own energetic blockages, or to let go of so much of what is holding you back. Once you become aware of the way in which the flow of energy works, you can also see how, as with my client who had the unhappy relationships (see p. 41), we all become our own self-fulfilling prophecy. Looking at the world in a more aware and meaningful way therefore leads you to a deeper understanding of what it really means to have the power to create your own reality at any given moment. We can energise our negative intentions in just the same way as we can our positive ones. If I suddenly decide that my world is no longer magical and looking gorgeous, but is in fact absolutely awful (which in miserable moments of course I sometimes do), then every little thing that happens seem to look awful. Instead of books arriving and parking spaces opening up, the rain falls, my washing gets wet, the dogs bring mud into the kitchen, my hips expand by two inches, and woe is me! Of course, those moments are nothing major, but I consciously make an effort to take a step back, return to my centre and say, 'Help!' And sure enough, the help comes, before I decide that things look even worse than they did just a moment earlier.

Even in those dark moments, the help that we think we want may not be the help we need; and so events can take such an unexpected turn that you're left wondering what on earth is actually happening. But sure enough, given time to unfold, everything happens exactly as it should. Seeing the world as magical or miserable is, of course, a matter of perception. So shifting your perception is crucial in determining the way that you will energise your intentions, and the kind of energies that you will attract back into your life. Years ago I was convinced that, wonderful though life was, it was my job to get up every day, heal the world by 5pm and then put my feet up for tea. Because I was working from a view that everyone and everything needed to be healed, all I saw were lots of people and animals that were looking for healing. Often this was really hard work for me, because of course, I was attracting a lot of needy people and animals into my life. Time went by and it dawned on me that actually I was not going to heal the world by 5pm at all. It

Almost everything you see about your own world is your own construct; the world is a mirror of how things are for you inside.

became apparent that, unless I was going to run around like a headless chicken constantly ministering to the sick, the easiest way to see myself as part of the world was to let go. I let go of choosing to see myself in this role, and just waited with an open

heart and mind and see what came. After a while, the work I was doing shifted, and I began to attract a different kind of energy into my life. People became less needy but more responsible for their own healing, and more supportive of each other. People came to work with me who were positive and optimistic about the shifts that are taking place in the world, and how wonderful the changes are.

Now, did the world change, or did I change my view of it? What I feel is that through my own process of healing, my view of the world changed, and so, in turn, the energy that I was attracting into my world changed. This reinforced the happier view, and the happier view attracted more peaceful energy. As your level of awareness steadily increases, it becomes apparent that almost everything you see about your own world is your own construct; that the world you see is a mirror of how things are for you inside. The term for this is 'reflection'; it's the concept that all external life is ultimately a mirror of your inner life.

I always find it amusing and enlightening just to listen to people as they talk about how they see the world in which they live. At one of my workshops a wonderful gentleman who had come to learn to do some hands-on work told me a story about an old man who was sitting on a park bench. A young man walked up to him and said, 'I'm moving into the next street, what are the neighbours like around here?' The old man asked him, 'What are the people like where you're from?' 'Horrible', said the young man. And the old man replied, 'Well, you know what? They're the same here.' Later on, a different young man approached the old man and asked the same question. 'I'm moving into the next street. What are people like around here?' 'Well', the old man asked again, 'What are they like where you're from?' 'Oh,' the young man responded, 'they're wonderful people.' The old man smiled and said, 'You know, they're the same here.'

It might sound as though I'm repeating the 'glass half-empty' lecture I gave in the first chapter. But what I'm trying to explain here is that the way in which people see the world is actually just a reflection of how they feel inside and that you can influence both your external and your internal realities by utilising your soul energy. At this point, you can actually look at the way in which you perceive your own life, and without judgement, make a choice to change the way you see that glass. Now that you know you have the power to touch your soul, and to find a place of gentleness, peace, and love whenever you want to, you can revisit that feeling and energise your intent to heal, or to let go of whatever pattern it is that you're stuck in, at any moment. You can always choose to see the glass as half-full. You can always choose to see yourself as a perfect expression of energy. Simply touch that still place, and let go. Look in the mirror that is your world, and tell the old man on the bench that all the people where you live are really wonderful. Even if you don't believe it at first, as I explained in the chapter on language and energy, you can begin to believe it by changing what you say. Tell people that you believe it; tell yourself that you believe it and the reality will create itself. I'm not suggesting here that you ignore reality, but that you change it.

NOTICING WHAT YOU NOTICE

So, working from the level of your soul energy helps to bring about and reinforce the momentum of loving and positive energy in your life with every thought you have about it. If you project energy and light from the level of your perfect soul, you will attract more energy and light back into your life. The snowball rolls down the mountain, the magical world is really real. The beauty of this process is that the more you look for the magic, the more magic you see. Something that I encourage people to do is to be aware of what they notice. If you always notice what needs healing, you're projecting your own need for healing outside; both reflecting and perpetuating your own reality. If you always notice love and magic and synchronicity, you're projecting your own feelings of love and synchronicity out into the world, which reflect and perpetuate that reality. Pay attention to what you notice about other people and ask yourself what you would rather see. If someone talks to me about how they feel people are not to be trusted, it's clear that this person's problem lies not only in trusting others, but also in trusting themselves. A colleague of mine recently did a lecture weekend for a woman who had told him at some length about all the charlatans, unprofessional people and fake healers she had come across. It later transpired that she found all kinds of excuses not to pay my colleague for his weekend's work. Clearly, she was the fake that she saw in other people and the whole situation arose from projecting her lack of trust and belief in herself, onto others. Take a

moment to look at what you're noticing about the world. If you don't like it, energise your intent to experience things differently.

GIVING WHAT YOU NEED

Trust and love are two of the deepest issues we face in our everyday lives, and ones that lie at the core of emotional and physical problems for so many people. They tend to be stumbling blocks in one form or another for a great many of us as part of the human experience: lack of trust and lack of love both call for a leap of faith in the person perceiving the lack, because it's an outer projection of their own inner state. In other words, if you notice a lack of love, you have a lack of love within you. If someone tells me that

Energise your intent to give and receive love, then take a step back and wait for the synchronicities to occur.

nobody loves them, it's clear to me that this is someone who needs to learn to love their own self first. There is undoubtedly love in the world; but perhaps that person isn't seeing it or accepting it. And of course, the key to learning to love or trust others, is to love or trust oneself first. A little bit of projected energy attracts more of the same and sets the snowball rolling down the

mountain. So, when you feel that sense of lack in yourself, go back to your soul, feel that sense of peace, and say, 'I am perfect'. And know that this is so. And know that the rest of the world is also perfect; see the perceived lack as an opportunity for healing. In noticing what you notice, you have given yourself the opportunity to recreate your own reality. Energise your intent to give and receive love, then take a step back and wait for the synchronicities to occur. These might take the form of opportunities to give love to others or receive love from them; or they might be opportunities to give love to yourself.

To actively attract more positive energy into your life, just give a little of what you feel you need. It's exactly the same principle as sowing a seed to grow a plant, and harvest twenty seeds. That's how nature multiplies upon itself; and because the creative energy that is the source at which we are all conjoined is simple, the rawest form of nature, it works in exactly the same way. Some spiritual teachers call it 'creating abundance' which some people tend to associate with 'money' or 'material gain'. I would apply this seed-sowing principle as simply attracting what you need into your life. Ultimately, nothing will come to you if it is not helpful to your life in some way. But do remember that this is a powerful

SOWING SEEDS TO ATTRACT WHAT YOU NEED INTO YOUR LIFE

A client of mine was a compulsive spender and deeply in debt as a result of amassing huge quantities of material possessions. He was constantly praying for the universe to help – which for him meant wanting more money so that he could pay off his debts. But there was also a level at which he was sincerely asking for help; and so what happened was that he lost his job. At the time he felt that this was the worst possible thing that could happen; he needed money and suddenly, his supply was cut off. Of course, his bank took away his overdraft facility, his credit card companies withdrew his credit, and he was utterly stuck. What happened was that he simply had to stop spending; and in no longer having the ability to spend, he learned that he could live without spending. He also learned that in fact he was no less happy not spending than he had been spending, and that by not spending, he had actually regained a measure of self-respect, self-love, and had little more ease and a little less fear in his life. He sincerely asked for help, and the help came; it wasn't the kind of help he thought he wanted, but it was certainly what he needed to heal his spending habit. Of course there was far more involved in his need to spend than the fact of just wanting to buy things, and as a result of his physical inability to spend, he was forced to address his inner needs and the drives that had led him to behave in this way. So his healing process began. By stating his intent to rid himself of debt, he was sowing a seed, and what he needed came.

Another way for him to have dealt with his problem could have been to stop energising the habit he needed to let go of. By simply choosing not to engage in the activity that was a problem for him, he would have withdrawn his energy from that process and the process would have ceased of itself. The more he thought of himself as a label – 'a compulsive spender' – the more he got into situations where he thought, 'I can't help it, I am a compulsive spender, I have to spend money.' Had he withdrawn his energy from that process earlier in the pattern, and returned to his centre to maintain a sense of peace, he would have ceased to energise the spending.

CASE STUDY

Every time you label yourself, or someone labels you, see yourself as perfect.

process and that, if you place your intent upon bringing you what you need, you will surely receive it. This is not meant to sound trite or superficial; I have worked with and seen this process working in what appeared to be some truly awful and desperate situations, and I know it to be true.

DE-ENERGISING TO RELEASE THE PATTERN

The process of de-energising a negative intent is useful in situations where you're really not sure what the positive intent really is, or where to place your intent. By choosing not to engage in a habit or process which we are energising in a perhaps uncomfortable way, we can change our reality by ceasing to give energy to that situation – by actively de-energising it. Of course, it's not always that simple with some of our more addictive habits.

De-energising is a powerful process for helping to release physical illness, too. So if, for example, I want to rid my body of a cold, I choose to see myself as a perfect soul, and return to my centre as often as possible to experience that sense of peace and strength. What people often do is address the cold and ask for it to be healed – but in so doing, they are energising the statement 'I have a cold'. Adding energy to a situation you would really rather release is something that happens all too often where chronic illness is concerned. I so often receive e-mails entitled, 'Cancer Patient' or, 'Lung Cancer', often without the subject's name, so that it's almost as if people identify so strongly with a label that the person with the illness *is* the illness. All this adds energy to a pattern that it would really be more helpful to release. So, if you have an illness, every time you think of your dis-ease, or label yourself, or someone else labels you, centre yourself within your soul energy and see yourself as perfect. Doing this regularly throughout the day is a deeply healing process that will withdraw your energy from reinforcing the label and help to energise your experience of yourself as a perfect being.

Labelling others – 'Oh, she's the cancer patient' – or adding energy to an expression of life, is something that each of us does all the time when we are in a low state of awareness. If you find yourself labelling someone else, this is also the time to return to your soul energy and realise that they, too are a perfect expression of creative soul energy. So often clients say to me, 'When I tell people about my condition, they treat me differently, and I hate it. I'm still the same person.' So, withdraw your energy from the process of judgement and see the perfection. De-energise the label; energise the perfect soul. Learning to see other people in this way is a deeply empowering process for them, too, as they are released on every energetic level of their existence from 'being the label'.

When working with some special needs clients recently, I found that the other therapists working with me were raising their voices and speaking in simplistic terms to all of the clients as a matter of course, in the way that some people speak to children. This was a clear-cut case of energising the 'difference' between the able-bodied among us and those with special needs. I refused to engage in that

process and little by little, the other therapists noticed that as I laughed and joked quite naturally with the clients, they responded in the same way that anyone else would have done. Of course, there was no difference between us.

ENERGISING OTHERS' SOULS
Withdrawing your energy from the label involves not engaging in the trivial or superficial 'stuff' that keeps people locked into their patterns. By treating them unconditionally, you are extending the most healing energy possible to another human being. An example of how so many of us tend to engage in the process of energising the label and energising the process of judgement is when we see someone behaving in a way that our egos tell us is unacceptable; for example, a man hitting his wife. Now this might be a hard one to swallow

Do nothing more than live from your soul energy and engage with others at that level.

a perfect being. This is the most powerfully healing way to be with another person. Not only are you withdrawing the energy from the label that energises the behaviour, but you are energising the level at which they are a perfect being, and thus actually helping that individual to live at soul level and release the pain that they are holding, too. This doesn't mean that you must condone the behaviour – simply see the soul behind it.

This unconditional way of being is the most simple, graceful way of healing that I know, and yet it is the strongest way too. I can think of countless situations where I have had the opportunity to witness and be part of this soul-level engagement and soul-level healing. So many people who participate in healing therapies think they actually have to 'do' something but in point of fact, you need do nothing more than live from your soul energy and engage with others at that level. So, clearly, the more time you spend centring yourself, the better equipped you will be to maintain that level of awareness and extend that peace to others. In turn, the more time you spend engaging with others at soul level, the more this energises your own sense of being within your soul-level energy and thus your own ongoing process of healing, too. When I say that I've been through enough of this in my

for some people, but that man, with his violence, anger, abuse and all, is as perfect a soul as his wife, and as perfect a soul as you and I. The man labelled 'violent' is expressing his own internal pain, turmoil, frustration and anger in much the same way that the child who stamps, and kicks and shouts 'I hate you'. So the only appropriate way to handle someone who engages in what you would label or judge to be violent, aggressive or otherwise unpleasant behaviour, is to de-energise the process that keeps them stuck. Allow your soul energy to engage with them at the level of their own soul, and to treat them as own life to know that what I'm telling you is a profoundly powerful process, I'm also giving you another example of magical synchronicity and a shifting perspective on living life. I could have said, 'I'm a victim. I've had a terrible life'; and in fact many people have said to me, 'Clare, you have had such a difficult time' during one situation or another. The level of difficulty, however, was in each individual's perception of the situation. As soon as you let go to be within your soul energy, the healing is allowed to happen.

You need do nothing more than let go and accept the process.

So, when the sickness comes, when you lose the job, when the relationship is on the rocks, and the bank withdraws your credit, don't throw your hands up in despair. Remember that there is a far more intelligent process at work here than you are aware of and that what you feel you want may not in fact be what you need. You may well be experiencing exactly what you need to right now, and it is very likely that this is a gift through which you are being given the opportunity to let your soul shine, and lead your life to where it really needs to be. You need

do nothing more than let go and accept the process. The more you let go and remain in your level of unconditional awareness, the more you will become aware of the signs that life is showing you before the crises occur.

In the next chapter, we'll take a practical look at synchronicity and maintaining your level of awareness, and the ways in which you can more actively follow the guidance offered to you in order to make the most of every opportunity that life brings. In this way you will begin to live your soul agenda for ongoing and long-term healing.

You have now learned how to shift the level of your own
awareness whenever you need to and work from the
energy of your soul, as well as how to harness that soul
energy to maintain the momentum of energetic movement
in your life. This is the process of aligning your soul agenda
with physical life. Walking your soul path is the clearest
way to maintaining your own healing and wellbeing on an

CHAPTER 7

Alignment

ongoing basis. It's about living from a position where you
have the peace to accept that your life is working out
perfectly, the awareness to see the guidance that life offers
you, and the strength to make a move or change when
necessary. This is the true meaning of taking up your soul
path and being able to live a healed life on a long-term
basis. Now let's take a look at how this works in practice.

GOING WITH THE FLOW

Living from your soul energy means moving with the flow of energy through your life and being the physical expression of your soul agenda at all times. This is an ongoing state of healing, and means that you can spot where to move and how to work with your life before a crisis – whether in your health, emotions, or relationships – occurs.

One of the easiest ways to get 'on flow' with the energy of your life is by taking a deeper but non-judgemental retrospective look at your own energetic pattern to see how you got to where you are. This will provide you with some clues about your own process.

CASE STUDY

GOING WITH THE FLOW

A student named Andrew came to one of my workshops having experienced what some of the others really felt was a most awful series of disasters. When he was four years old, his mother had died of liver cancer. His father tried for a little while working part-time and caring for his children, but could not bring in enough money to keep the family at the same time as trying to care for them himself. So, following a somewhat traumatic parting when Andrew was nearly six years old, the three children were sent hundreds of miles away to live with their aunt. Andrew and his sisters rarely saw their father because of the distance between them, and they struggled to adjust to their new life. Although the care and standard of living the children had with their aunt and uncle in a rural home were conducive to a supportive upbringing and generally happy way of living, Andrew never really got over the sense that his father had abandoned them. However, he had a happy school life and studied a wide variety of subjects, focusing in particular on science and nature. The home he was raised in gave him ample opportunity to spend time outdoors with all kinds of animals, and Andrew eventually went to college to train in veterinary medicine.

He began a successful career as a vet and became a partner in a veterinary practice, specialising in horses. He married and had a family of his own. Andrew became increasingly absorbed in his work, as he was very conscious of wanting to be the good provider he felt his own father had never been. He wanted his family to have plenty of money and to be able to buy or do anything that they should need or want. What he didn't bargain for was that, in spending all of his time at work, Andrew was simply playing the role of the absent father to his own young family. After some years and many struggles within the relationship, Andrew's wife left him for another man, taking their children with her.

Andrew was devastated, and began to drink heavily. Inevitably his much-valued working life began to suffer, as he was unable to remain sober enough to carry out his duties. As his fear over his dwindling income and impending divorce increased, so did his drinking habit. Eventually, his partners asked him to leave the veterinary practice that had been such a treasured part of his life, and Andrew came out of his marriage and his career in poor health, financially desolate and deeply depressed. At this point, Andrew was diagnosed with a cancerous tumour on his liver; the same disease that had killed his mother.

He had reached what could only be described as the darkest night his soul had ever experienced. For the first few weeks after his tumour was diagnosed, he refused to even acknowledge that there was anything wrong with him. He told me that in retrospect, he feels this was because he was in a state of limbo where he really wasn't sure whether he wanted to live or die. Then one day, out of the blue, a client who did not know that he had left his practice telephoned him at home to tell him about her horse, which he had advised be put to sleep due to an inoperable and incurable bone disease. 'It's just incredible,' she said, with great enthusiasm. 'I found this guy who works with healing energy, and the horse is fine – he's back in work. Can you believe it? I'd love you to come and see for yourself.'

The client in question happened to be someone with whom Andrew had spent a great deal of time because of her horse's ill health, and with whom he had discussed alternative methods of therapy when it became clear that conventional medicine had nothing more to offer. He was happy to have a reason to go out and to take an interest in the horse's recovery, and, having seen the horse well and fit, Andrew was inspired to get in

CASE STUDY

touch with the healing practitioner who had cured the horse for help with his own cancer. This was the beginning of Andrew's recovery, and the point at which his life took a dramatic turn for the better.

Andrew first addressed his own health; he totally changed his approach to his diet and nutritional regime, and took responsibility for his own wellbeing. He began to meditate and visualise his tumour shrinking. He had regular healing sessions and attended training days to learn a wide variety of self-healing techniques. His cancer went into remission and, inspired by his own healing and backed by his medical knowledge, Andrew began to practise healing and holistic healthcare advice for horse owners. He has remarried and has a new family, with a wife who also works in complementary care. He now describes his life as 'better in every way than he could ever have dreamed possible'.

Now, it would be easy for anyone to look at Andrew's story and say that he had indeed suffered a terrible life. Another approach would be to see the synchronicity that brought him to the point that he's at now. This is how Andrew sees his own process: his mother's death gave him an interest in medicine from an early age; and his move to a rural home enabled him to spend time with animals, so that his chosen career was to become an equine veterinary surgeon. The way he felt about his own father led him to manage his own family life in a way that contributed to his marriage, career and health breaking down. He says, 'Had I been more aware, I would have realised that I was destroying myself. I would have also explored complementary medicine long before, as I'd always had an interest in natural methods, but my colleagues and family would never have supported my interest. So in point of fact, it was right for me to leave both situations; though I would never have done so by choice. My own illness gave me the opportunity to experience the power of working with energy for myself. The horse that led me to the healer was one of the reasons why I used to spend a lot more time at work than I should have done; so he has really done me a favour. That was the healer who I took my first classes from and who started my study of ways to work with energy. The whole thing has been a flow of events leading me to the right place in my life. I could have had it much easier, had I been more honest with myself instead of constantly compromising what I felt I wanted to do, and doing what people expected of me.'

Andrew says that he now takes great care to remain aware of the signs his life is showing him so that, instead of going through so much trauma next time, he will be able to live his soul agenda and simply flow with the energy of his life. Instead of seeing challenges as fearful situations to be avoided, he embraces them as opportunities for a new experience and growth. So, for example, if someone brings a horse to him that he would formerly have said should be put to sleep, he will spend time, with his wife, discussing and researching the possibilities to find other ways to care for the animal's health. If he has a series of cases with the same condition, he realises that he needs to learn more about how to care for that condition. If he receives a request to travel to a distant part of the country to visit a client, he goes, and sees where the opportunity takes him. He continually reaffirms his intent in doing whatever it is he needs to do to live his life from soul level, and follows the signs that life shows him from a level of higher awareness.

Andrew is a wonderful example of someone who lives his life with the peace and energy that enable him to exist with real meaning. As a result, his health is blooming and his personal life is happy and full. Had he chosen to be aware of the signs his life was showing him, he could have avoided the series of crises he experienced – that's certainly his aim now, given his past experiences. Even when an apparently difficult situation faces him, he goes with it, trusting that this will take him to a new level of learning and healing. In the past, as he said, he was too busy being what he felt other people wanted him to be. Had he followed his own integrity, he could have given himself the opportunity to explore the natural methods of healthcare he was interested in while he was married the first time and within his veterinary practice. It is possible that he could have brought his new knowledge to both of those situations and integrated it. It is also possible that, had he genuinely felt his life was taking him in another direction, he could have left his practice before being forced to.

SYNCHRONICITY AND YOUR LIFE

I have heard countless stories of events, or strings of events that have led people to fulfilling their true purpose and being in life. Many of us have to go through some really challenging experiences before we wake up enough to see what life is trying to show us, Often, although we can see where a series of events is leading us, and also see ways out of a situation at many different junctures, we ignore the signs because we are so locked into our own limited view

Each of us needs to remain centred enough within our own sense of awareness.

of what we 'should' be and do. But it is important to remember that within every challenge, there is a synchronicity that the flow of energy within our lives is leading us through.

SEEING THE SIGNS

We have to learn to see the signs, and sadly, sometimes that comes through our experiencing a truly dark night of the soul as a wake-up call. Each of us needs to remain centred enough within our own sense of awareness to follow the flow of energy within our lives. That may mean that we take action, it may mean that we simply accept the ways

things are and work with them. Following the guidance we receive means accepting the fact that there may be something else we can learn, something else we can do, or another direction in which we could look. The guidance that each of us receives can be as simple as, for example, following up on a chance meeting with someone to see what we can share or learn from each other, or what each of us has to bring to the other's experience of life. It can be a question of staying aware of what it is you are noticing about other people, and seeing how this is a projection of something that you need to address as part of your own process of letting go and energising your life more positively. It can be about seeing how the way that you lived as a child, or the experiences you have learned from your parents, have given you strengths and abilities that you can use now.

Guidance often comes to us in the form of animals. The changes that occur within the earth's magnetic field are very tangible to animals because they don't have the same complicated experience of their existences that we do. This has become a favourite subject for me because a great many of the people I meet and work with have experienced steep learning curves and profound life changes for the better through having certain animals enter their lives. My own learning has always been shaped by the animals with whom I am privileged to share my life. Often, the sickness an animal experiences will be enough to propel its owner along a path of learning and self-discovery.

Don't engage in the process of sign-spotting at an ego-level and begin analysing every little occurrence in your life; simply remain aware and see what happens.

As I said in chapter five on meditation, don't take all of this too seriously. Don't engage in this process of sign-spotting at an ego-level and begin analysing every little occurrence in your life; simply remain aware and see what happens next. I have some very sweet but rather over-zealous students who once took me so literally on this point that on one occasion, following a weekend workshop, I received a full fortnight's worth of e-mails on what people had noticed. They started out with, 'I have seen a fox – what does this mean?'. This was followed by, 'yes – I, too, have seen a fox. Two foxes. What does that mean?' and then, 'I saw a dog, and three cats. What is life telling me?' and so on. Sure, you can read up on the symbolism of dogs and cats and foxes. It's fascinating stuff and you can learn a great deal from it. But there also comes a point at which you can also just accept that there are dogs and cats and foxes!

The kind of flag-waving that life does for you that is meaningful, clear and easy to follow is when, for example, you suddenly notice several references within days or a week of each other to a certain person – this is, of course, how synchronicity works. Often people get in touch with me because someone mentioned a healing therapy, someone else mentioned my name, and someone then gave that person a book of mine. They telephone me saying, 'It looks like I should come and see you!' This was how my move to another part of the country came about; a series of people in my life were from that area, a series of events led to my husband wanting to move back to the area he was from, and so on. I could have dug my heels in and said, 'No! We will stay where we are, and we will make things work here!' But in point of fact, I saw the signs and said, 'OK, let's go with it.' Since we moved, things have begun to unfold so very rapidly that the flow of life that I was moseying along with before has been exchanged for something like a torrent that I'm rafting on!

Your dreams are your mind's way of raising your awareness of the way you see and feel about the world.

Living your soul agenda means following the signs that life shows you and exploring the ways that the flow of energy and synchronicity in your life seem to be suggesting that you go. The process does not always take you where you think it will, or should; in fact in some cases it seem to lead you right back to where you've come from, but gives you a new approach and some learned experience to refresh your view of your way of living.

USING YOUR DREAMS

One of the ways in which the human mind waves a flag about unconscious issues, or simply finds ways for your conscious mind to notice what you're perhaps not consciously noticing in your life, is through your dreams. Full of thoughts and feelings that are translated into stories, pictures and symbols, your dreams are your mind's way of raising your awareness of the way you see and feel about the world. There are no hard and fast rules about what anything that you dream actually 'means', although there are all kinds of books offering different explanations. There is simply a language of symbols and pictures that your mind will give you to help you understand what it is aware of and that you perhaps would consciously be as well to become more aware of.

Analysing and interpreting your dreams is not even the job, necessarily, of an expert in dream analysis and interpretation; because whoever interprets your dreams will interpret them from their perspective, and with their view of the world, rather than your own. Sometimes, it's simply a question of writing down your dream and allowing yourself to reflect over whatever comes to mind when you go through it. This could be feelings, memories, or ideas about something you need or want to do, or somewhere you would like to go. You might have some thoughts about something you did the previous day, or someone you talked to. Often, whatever comes to you in the process of abstract thinking about your sense of the dream is as accurate as any interpretation that someone else could give you.

Remember that there is no right or wrong, and there is nothing to judge. Go with anything that comes into your head related to the dreams you are having, and note how you feel. The thoughts and feelings that you have will, in turn, lead you to whatever it is that you need to become consciously aware of. It could be something you did yesterday that you are upset about, or perhaps you're very excited about going to meet someone today, or maybe you're coming to terms with losing a close member of your family a few years ago. Just notice what you feel and when you become uncomfortable with what you're experiencing, bring your sense of soul peace to that feeling. The whole process of raising

There is no right and wrong and there is nothing to judge. Go with anything that comes into your head related to the dreams you are having.

awareness can peel away so many layers of your onion that, feelings of discomfort are transformed by your soul energy to a healed place of peace. Becoming aware of what your dreams are telling you that your unconscious mind, or your other levels of awareness, perhaps, notice, or feel, or think about, gives you the opportunity to let go on an even deeper level and move with the flow of energy in your life.

Most people, at some point in their lives, face a crossroads, where the signs seem to be pointing in two different directions at the same time.

One lovely example of how a dream can unravel what the various levels of your awareness know is one in which a student of mine came to terms with the death of her father. In her dream, she was trying to rescue him from a terrible disaster, and bring him back to life. As her dream ended, she had the clear thought that there was absolutely nothing more she could do to help him. Afterwards, when she processed her feelings, she became aware that in the years since her father's death, she had carried with her a nagging sense that there was something more she could have done, or should have done, to help him before he died. Her dream was not only symbolic of her need to let go, but was also a healing in itself in that it enabled her to release the pattern of worry and guilt she had carried with her since her father's death. She felt a great sense of relief following the dream, forgave herself, and accepted the process.

SELF-OBSERVATION

Sometimes, despite our willingness to remain centred and aware, the signs we see might be none too clear. Most people, at some point in their lives, face a crossroads, where the signs seem to be pointing in two different directions at the same time. We have all had times when we sense we are experiencing an opening up of paths, or feel a need to change direction, and it's at this point that we worry about the pros and cons of the situation, which decision is the right one to make, and so on. A great deal of time, effort, energy, and angst can be invested in this kind of dilemma. We might make up our minds, only to change them again; or start to move in one direction, only to find that it's not what we thought it would be, and then want to backtrack. We might seek advice from friends and relatives, and still be none the wiser.

Alternatively, by remaining with your energy at soul level, you can simply detach from the need to do anything at all, and just wait to see what comes to you, or what signs life shows you, or in which direction life takes you. You can guarantee that, if you are struggling to see a sign or make a decision, then it is not the right time for the decision to be made. It is this level of soul awareness at which you can stay in a position of dynamic peace. You can remain alert to the possibility that you may need to move when the signs become clearer, moving with the flow and change of energy and events, yet aware enough to see where life is leading you and engage your energy in the shifts and changes that are working in your life. This is the way in which to maintain the momentum of healing and live in a state of true peace and fulfilment.

Living a fulfilled life is not about being a label or identifying yourself with a job or role; nor is it about material gain, meeting other people's expectations, or helping anyone other than yourself. It's about achieving nothing more than a deep and sincere letting go. Nobody expects a healed life to be one that remains in a state of perfect bliss all the

time. It's all right to feel down sometimes, to have the odd bad day, and just accept that this is how things are, for the time being. Beating yourself up, saying, 'But I

It's all right to feel down sometimes, to have the odd bad day, and just accept that this is how things are, for the time being.

must be happy!' is only likely to produce inner conflict and stress. If the crisis occurs, and you move through it, this is just life's way of taking you most purposefully in a given direction. It's probably happened because you were so engrossed in running the treadmill that you didn't take time out to notice what was happening before it happened. But accept the crisis as a gift with which you can expand your own awareness, and in future you won't need it in order to sit up and take notice of where life is taking you. Ultimately, following where life is taking you is truly living your soul agenda; simply being whatever you need to be, whenever you need to be it.

A good way to continue to place your energy within your own experience of life at soul level is to periodically return to your centre

Self-observation is something we can all practise. It only takes seconds out of a given situation and continually strengthens the process of centring ourselves within our deeper awareness and soul energy.

and observe yourself. Detachment is a perfect tool to use for self-observation. When I talk about observing yourself, I don't mean self-analysis. (Although it can be a positive process, self-analysis can become deeply destructive and is often a waste of time and energy.) By self-observation I mean standing back, seeing how you handled, perceived or behaved in a given process in your life, and, without

judgement, looking at what the outcome was.

Self-observation is something we can all practise. It only takes seconds out of a given situation and continually strengthens the process of centring ourselves within our deeper awareness and soul energy. As a simple rule of thumb, whenever you feel confused or uncomfortable, simply centre yourself, take a few deep breaths and stand back. Look at what you're doing and ask, 'Is this useful to me?' If it isn't, then without judgement, simply withdraw your energy from the process and cease to energise that pattern. If you feel as though you want to repeat the process, even if it feels somewhat strange, then go with it and place your energetic intent within whatever it is you're experiencing. If your intent is that you move with the direction that the energy is taking you in, then that positive intent will attract more energy to itself as a matter of course, and the process will unfold in a manner that may be deeply enlightening to you.

DE-ENERGISING THE PAST;
ENERGISING THE FUTURE
Healing on an ongoing basis and allowing your soul agenda to be truly fulfilled usually means letting go of the past. Not just once or twice, but continually, because the cycles of behaviour that we keep ourselves

trapped in are habits we learned in the past. You can choose to de-energise past cycles by actively engaging your energy in an intention to just Be. The actions that we repeat and the thoughts that we have are based on what we have already learned. So, instead of energising a pattern that is known to you, possibly even to the extent that it feels in some sense automatic and 'right' for you, you need to follow the signs that life is showing you and flow with the energy, to explore a new possibility.

Feelings of discomfort or unfamiliarity need not signal that you should beat a hasty retreat. Sometimes it's just that what's happening is not something you already know, and it doesn't feel right because it is not in line with your past experience. That's fine. That's what exploring new possibilities, growth and change are all about. So, in practical terms, to allow your soul agenda to truly come into being you have an instantly accessible facility to bring your soul energy to the fore and explore the possibilities and opportunities that life is showing you. All you have to do is centre yourself, detach, and ask, 'Is the reason I'm avoiding this just because it's unfamiliar?' If it is, so long as what you're being faced with is within your integrity – in other words, is not going harm you or anyone else – then just explore it.

You can choose to de-energise past cycles by actively engaging your energy in an intention to just Be.

I always feel that exploring new possibilities is the perfect way to release the past 'baggage' that we carry with us and continue to peel away the layers of our own onions. In the long term, such an ongoing process of release and centring is the clearest way to be within your soul energy and to fulfil, every day, the agenda that you need to live to maintain a fulfilled and healthy experience of life. In practical terms, the habit of releasing the past and moving into your soul energy is such a liberating experience that your own process gains momentum

Expanding your way of being and exploring how it feels to energise a new pattern instead of an old one are the keys.

purely through the joy and excitement of exploring new possibilities and releasing some of what was holding you back. It's a little bit like a spiritual diet – the first few pounds you lose give you such a huge incentive to lose more, that your enthusiasm and confidence are boosted by each little shift of the scales. In terms of your own healing, you will find that your enthusiasm and confidence are boosted by each little withdrawal of energy from a past process that is no longer useful, and by each little energising of a

process of expansion and exploration.

Confidence is, of course, one of the key factors in daring to explore something new. The easiest way to begin to gain confidence in your own healing process is to treat the first step as a risk that what you know might not necessarily be the only way. Perhaps what you think of as 'right' is exactly what has been creating the patterns that you want to release. Expanding your way of being and exploring how it feels to energise a new pattern instead of an old one are the keys. Releasing an old pattern to discover that a new one is actually more pleasurable is the best way to gain confidence and, of course, the only way to discover which is the more pleasurable process is to take the opportunities that life gives you to explore. For example, if someone approaches you with an idea that is completely new to you, such as 'Would you like to try crystal therapy?' – just say, 'Yes!'

So many people say that they 'want to be how they were before' a sickness, or crisis in their lives. The whole point about healing is that you don't go back to the old pattern, simply to jump back on the carousel and end up in the same place again. The point is that you jump off the carousel, and try walking forwards instead of continually going round and round. It's a small leap to make, but it can free you from the whole energy cycle you're currently in. After all, if it's too scary out there, you can always jump back on again.

FORGIVENESS – AN EXERCISE IN HEALING

Forgiveness is a big part of living your soul agenda. Letting go and making the leap into new experiences means forgiving on an ongoing basis. You forgive yourself for whatever you are judging yourself to be; for example, for staying with an old pattern for so long, or for not seeing the signs before. You forgive those around you for any perceived issues you might be holding against them. Forgiveness is not about being gracious by letting yourself or someone else off for doing something awful. It's about withdrawing judgement from the whole process. You can make an ongoing choice to de-energise the process of judgement and not engage in holding any of your own, or other people's past actions or deeds against yourself or them. In itself, de-energising the process of judgement is a deeply liberating and healing process because it leaves more energy available with which to live and explore new opportunities as they occur.

Sometimes it can help to take any held issues into a meditation, or just with you into your soul energy and consciously energise the decision to let go of that pattern. For example, Andrew (see p136) spent a lot of time being angry with the partners of his veterinary practice for asking him to leave instead of supporting him. So, to help himself de-energise his judgement process, he sat down and held an image of the moment at which he was asked to leave, and the sense of anger he felt in his mind. Then, he centred himself in his soul energy and held the visual image with him, going through all the feelings he held, the thoughts he had about what should or should not have been said and done, and the words that actually were said, until the feelings of anger subsided. This exercise took him

'Would you like to try crystal therapy?' – just say, 'Yes!'

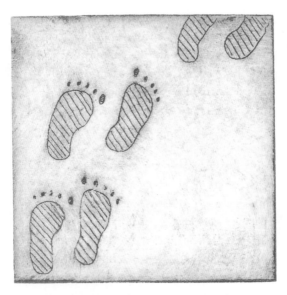

Hold the images that are associated with your feelings in your mind, centre yourself within your soul energy and stay centred.

other than an affection and respect for these people as human beings. His energy is free to work forwards, instead of constantly lagging behind. This exercise can be applied to anything you find that you are judging yourself for, whether in specific situations – 'I shouldn't have shouted at my husband last week, I feel bad about it' – or in more general terms, - 'I wish I was a more loving person'. Hold the images that are associated with your feelings in your mind, centre yourself within your soul energy, and stay centred as you allow all the events, words and feelings related to your particular issue in your mind. Stay there until you reach a sense of peace and the thoughts or images are simply no longer a problem. It's a liberating process and one you can repeat as often as you feel necessary, or even as part of your daily meditation, to continually let go of energy that is invested in anything other than living your soul agenda fully and freely.

around thirty minutes to complete and at the end of the process, he no longer felt angry; he had just let go. As a result he now faces his former work colleagues on a regular basis with no feeling of past energy

LIVING YOUR SOUL AGENDA

In terms of living your soul agenda, here are some key points that you can work with:

Centre yourself within your soul energy frequently. Engage with others at soul level and de-energise useless labels. At any given moment during the day, stop what you are doing and ask yourself: Am I doing this because it makes me happy? Do I feel at peace? If not, how do you feel? Are you sad, worried, angry, tense?

With detachment, look back and see the synchronicity of your life as it is now; where the synchronicity of events has transpired to lead you, and how, right up to the present moment. Observe yourself, whatever you're engaged in doing and ask, 'Is this what I always do? Can I do something differently to break the cycle?'

Remain aware of the meaningful synchronicities that life offers you in dreams, people you meet, what animals show you, and so on. Follow guidance and signs along your path to explore the possibility of energising a new process.

Accept that you will have the odd 'down' times. Treat challenge as an opportunity to explore.

Actively de-energise past patterns to release energy that may be trapped there and is no longer serving you. Allow yourself to move with the flow of energy in your life. If you really don't know what to do, just remain centred and trust that the way will become clear. Re-affirm your intent to move with the flow of energy in your life, and consciously energise your healing process on an ongoing basis.

This is the practical way to truly walk your soul path; the way to do and be whatever it is that you really came here to do and be. This is the way to maintain long-term health, energy and peace. It is likely that your life will begin to unfold in ways that you could never have imagined possible!

My hope is that this book will have helped you to engage in the process of living your soul agenda, to bring healing into your life on a long-term basis. Bringing our soul energy, the perfect essence that we truly are, into line with our physical life, is the responsibility that each of us has to ourselves as part of our own process of expansion. Ultimately, all any of us needs to do with our lives is to move with the energy that takes us where we need to be at any given time. Healing others will take place naturally, simply because by healing yourself you make available to others a higher frequency of energy and a beacon of peace and soul by which they can learn. In raising our own

Final Words

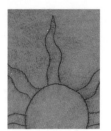

consciousness, we each have a part to play in raising the consciousness of the planet; of truly bridging the gap between heaven and earth. That's what the age we're living in is all about. By simply learning to honour the soul in others, each of us can go a long way toward raising consciousness on a global level. It is an exciting time in which to live and one in which each of us can play our own personal part in the next stage of man's evolution through awareness and the human journey.

It is not an overstatement to say that soul-level healing work is an intrinsic part of the next stage of man's development and evolution. Man is actively engaged in the search for a higher consciousness, and the shift in our awareness that our physical evolution and the development of the human brain is leading us towards, is all part of that process. In time I would like to see a move away from using the word 'healing' for this process, as it's simply a natural one of expansions and energetic shifts!

The whole point of our current phase of existence is to unclutter and simplify mankind's existence and realise (real-ise!) the fact that each of us is already in a state of existence that we might loosely call heaven. It's not somewhere we have to get to because we're already there; each of us is part of it at a very basic level, and each of us can be there at any time, should we choose to be so.

In the shift towards living from a higher level of consciousness, man is almost moving full circle to the point of living in the ultimate state of awareness – back to the source energy from which we came, perhaps? It's as if our foray into egotism and materialism has been a glitch on the path. A glitch, maybe, but a necessary one. Or, are we simply moving through the cycle of exploration and growth that has brought us towards a change? Are we moving back to a more natural state of being, or forward to a new state of existence? My feeling is that we are expanding and growing towards a whole new

The whole point of our current phase of existence is to unclutter and simplify mankind's existence.

plane of being. We may even be heading full circle, but ending up a little farther on than where we left off, because in point of fact, time and space are both relative issues and so there is no beginning or end, simply a level of awareness of existence.

It is said that at the moment man attains a truly enlightened state, he returns to the condition of the source energy from which he came. There are also theories that we will evolve to the point of no longer needing to exist in physical form, and will move on to a purely energetic existence. We have a long way to go yet to discover which turns out to be the case, but it's enjoying the process that is important. Following the path as it unfolds before us and living every moment to the full is all that any of us can aim to do. This is the path of your soul, and this is the path of healing and wholeness.

Index

Thanks

To my wonderful parents, thank you so much for giving me life and loving me so ceaselessly. To Daddy, the truest healer, who always sees the good in every soul, and the magical Mummy of the silver ray.

For my dearest, fathomless, most mystical and infinitely complex husband, Lee, whom I love from the depths of my being and beyond. Without you, there would be no me.

To Linda, and all the other Lindas – you know which one you are! Thank you for always looking out for me and for the peace you all so sweetly bring.

To the wonderful Wafties, Woollam, the Beans and the interplanetary Giles, Jan Benson, Lesley Gowers, Penny (Mrs Turner!), Barbara, Fyshe, Neenar, Di, the flying northern souls and Dharma. Everywhere you are, thank you all for your love, nurturing, support and for making me part of your lives. I am so truly blessed.

To my garden! For my orange boys: the gracious Daws Ace of Hearts and the unearthly Daws Jack of Hearts, we have so much to DO! For dearest Pip, my guardian and chaperone, Dill the wizard and amazing Daizy, familiars and angels all.

Contacts

Clare Wilde can be contacted by e-mail at:
wilde@naturalhealing.co.uk.

For colour flower essences: Paullambillion@dial.pipex.com.

E-mail discussion list run by some of Clare's students:
wafties@egroups.com.

Bibliography and Recommended reading

A Course in Miracles, the Foundation for Inner Peace, Viking Penguin

Bach Flower Therapy (Theory & Practice), Mechthild Scheffer, Thorsons

The Fragrant Heavens (The Spiritual Dimension of Fragrance and Aromatherapy), Valerie Ann Worwood, Doubleday

Gems and Crystals for Beginners, Kristyna Arcarti, Hodder & Stoughton

Healing with Colour, Theo Gimbel, Gaia Books Ltd

Healing Sounds (The Power of Harmonics), Jonathan Goldman, Element Books

If it hurts, it isn't love, Chuck Spezzano, Hodder & Stoughton

The Infinite Way, Joel Goldsmith, H.T. Hamblin, Bosham, Chichester

Jonathan Livingston Seagull, Richard Bach, HarperCollins

Kundalini and the Chakras (A Practical Manual), Genevieve Lewis Paulson, Llewellyn Publications, Minnesota (tel. 55164-0383)

Quantum Healing, Deepak Chopra, Bantam Books

The Tao of Food, Richard Craze and Roni Jay, Godsfield Press

The Tao of Physics, Fritjof Capra, Flamingo Books, HarperCollins

The Yoga Cookbook (Vegetarian Food for Body & Mind), Recipes from the Sivananda Yoga Vedanta Centres, Gaia Books Ltd

365 Tao Daily Meditations, Deng Ming Dao, HarperCollins, San Francisco

You can Heal your Life, Louise Hay, Hay House

Recommended Listening

The Raj tapes: www.nwffacim.org

For crystals, essential oils, healing music CDs and books: David
   Weldon at Insight, 12a, Florence Walk, North Street, Bishops
   Stortford, Herts, (tel. 01279 503740)

For books: The Speaking Tree, 5, High Street, Glastonbury, Somerset,
   (tel. 01458 835974)